PRAGMATICS

IN THE SAME SERIES

Editor: Richard Hudson

PRAGMATICS

Jean Stilwell Peccei

London and New York

First published 1999
by Routledge
11 New Fetter Lane, London EC4P 4EE

Simultaneously published in the USA and Canada
by Routledge
29 West 35th Street, New York, NY 10001

Routledge is an imprint of the Taylor & Francis Group

© 1999 Jean Stilwell Peccei

Typeset in Times Ten by The Florence Group,
Stoodleigh, Devon

Printed and bound in Great Britain by
TJ International Ltd, Padstow, Cornwall

British Library Cataloguing in Publication Data
A catalogue record for this book is available from the British Library

Library of Congress Cataloging in Publication Data
Peccei, Jean Stilwell.
 Pragmatics / Jean Stilwell Peccei.
 p. cm. — (Language workbooks)
 Includes bibliographical references and index.
 1. Pragmatics. I. Title. II. Series.
P99.4.P72P43 1999
306.44–dc21 99–10322
CIP

ISBN 0–415–20523–9

CONTENTS

For Patch

USING THIS BOOK

This workbook has been written for all those who are embarking on
the study of pragmatics for the first time and have little or no prior
background in linguistics. Because of this, technical terminology has
been kept to a minimum. Where specialist terms have been intro-
duced, they are explained in the text. You will find them highlighted
as KEY WORDS. As you will see in **Unit 1**, pragmatics is primarily   **Key word**
concerned with what speakers mean rather than what words or sen-
tences mean. For the sake of brevity, the use of *speaker* in these units
also includes *writer* and the use of *hearer* also includes *reader*.

You should not need to do any supplementary reading while you
are working your way through this book. However, the **Further
Reading** section at the end of each unit will provide you with suggested background reading and the sources for the research and data
which we will be discussing in the units.

Unit 1 explores the relationship between semantics and pragmatics,
the two branches of linguistics that look at meaning. **Units 2–9** cover
some of the basic techniques and key concepts involved in studying
and analysing pragmatic meaning. As you work through these units
you will find a number of exercises. Each **Exercise** is followed by a
Comment section with a solution to the problem posed by the data
and a further discussion of the topic under consideration. This workbook takes a 'hands on' approach to studying language, and you will
get much more out of the units if you complete each exercise before
moving on to the **Comment** section. At the end of **Units 1–8** you will
find **Further Exercises** which will give you the chance to practise and
consolidate your skills. Answers to these exercises appear at the end
of the workbook. All the units also have **Supplementary Exercises**
and **Discussion Questions** which allow for more independent work.
These exercises and questions do not have model answers, and if you
are not using this book as part of a taught course, you may find it
helpful to discuss your answers with someone else.

By the time you finish the first nine units, I hope that you will want to take your newly acquired skills into the real world. **Unit 10** provides you with ideas and guidance for carrying out several short research projects involving pragmatic analysis.

ACKNOWLEDGEMENTS

I owe many thanks to my students at Roehampton Institute who were the guinea pigs for many of the exercises used in the units, and to the series editor, Professor Richard Hudson, for his advice on writing for 'beginners' in linguistics. His comments, as always, have been invaluable, and any remaining mistakes and shortcomings are entirely mine. And last but not least, I would like to thank my editors at Routledge, Louisa Semlyen, Miranda Filbee and Diana Railton for their unfailing support and patience while I was writing this workbook.

ACKNOWLEDGEMENTS

WHAT IS PRAGMATICS?

1

> We explore the different meanings of *meaning* and the kinds of issues which are dealt with by semantics and pragmatics.

What do these children still need to learn about using language?

> A little boy comes in the front door.
> Mother: Wipe your feet, please.
> He removes his muddy shoes and socks and carefully wipes his clean feet on the doormat.

> A father is trying to get his 3-year-old daughter to stop lifting up her dress to display her new underwear to the assembled guests.
> Father: We don't DO that.
> Daughter: I KNOW, Daddy. You don't WEAR dresses.

The children's knowledge of vocabulary and grammar does not appear to be the problem. When the little boy's mother asked him to wipe his feet, that is exactly what he did. The little girl explained why her father was not participating in the underwear show with perfect grammar and quite impeccable logic. The problem is that the children appear to have understood what the words meant but not what their parents meant. As adults, we usually arrive at the speaker's meaning so effortlessly that we tend to be unaware of the considerable amount of skill and knowledge that we used to accomplish this.

Semantics and pragmatics are the two main areas of linguistic study that look at the knowledge we use both to extract meaning when we hear or read, and to convey meaning when we speak or write. Within linguistics itself, the dividing line between these two

Semantics
Pragmatics

disciplines is still under considerable debate. However, generally speaking, SEMANTICS concentrates on meaning that comes from purely linguistic knowledge, while PRAGMATICS concentrates on those aspects of meaning that cannot be predicted by linguistic knowledge alone and takes into account knowledge about the physical and social world. As you work through the exercises in this unit, you should be able to fill out these preliminary definitions a bit more and get a feel for what pragmatic analysis involves.

If you were counting, you will have noticed that the words *mean* and *meaning* have appeared 11 times so far and with several different meanings (12!). We will start our study of pragmatics by exploring the meaning (13!) of *meaning* (14!).

EXERCISE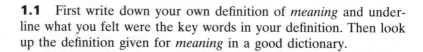

1.1 First write down your own definition of *meaning* and underline what you felt were the key words in your definition. Then look up the definition given for *meaning* in a good dictionary.

Comment

Did you get very far? Was the dictionary any help when it provided you with *purpose, significance, signification, intention* and *sense*? Let's try to break the task down into more manageable chunks. We will start with an important kind of knowledge for successfully interpreting language – word meaning.

EXERCISE

1.2 (a) What does *cat* mean? (b) What does *cream* mean? (c) What does to *drink* mean?

Comment

You probably found this fairly easy. My answers were: (a) *cat* a domestic feline; (b) *cream* the liquid fat of milk; (c) *drink* to consume liquid.

Lexical semantics

By providing definitions for individual words, you were analysing the kind of meaning that is the focus of LEXICAL SEMANTICS. Did you notice how you had to resort to the meanings of other words in the language in order to construct your definitions? Of course, providing word meanings is not always an easy task, nor is teaching them for that matter. An American high school teacher asked her students what *dogmatic* meant and received the following answer: *A machine powered by dogs.*

1.3   What does *Cats drink cream* mean?

Comment

Paraphrase

This was a bit more complicated, but still pretty manageable. When asked what a sentence means, people usually provide another sentence that has virtually the same meaning, a PARAPHRASE. There are a variety of ways that you could paraphrase *Cats drink cream.* You could change (a) individual words (b) the sentence structure, or (c) both the individual words and the sentence structure. Here are some possible paraphrases for our sentence:

> *Domestic felines consume the liquid fat of milk.*
> *Cream is drunk by cats.*
> *The liquid fat of milk is drunk by domestic felines.*

Sentence semantics

In this exercise you were carrying out the kind of analysis that is the focus of SENTENCE SEMANTICS. To provide a paraphrase you used your knowledge of the meanings of the individual words but you also used your knowledge of English grammar. For example, word order is very important for establishing sentence meaning in English. The sentences *Cats chase mice* and *Mice chase cats* contain the same words but have entirely different meanings.

✎ **EXERCISE**

1.4   Mike, Annie and Mike's cat, Felix, are in Mike's kitchen. What did Annie mean?

> Mike: What happened to that bowl of cream?
> Annie: Cats drink cream.

Comment

Now things have become considerably more complicated. We are no longer talking simply about what words or sentences mean, but what a person means as well. We have entered the realm of pragmatics and yet another meaning of *meaning.* It seems to me that in addition to saying that cream is drunk by cats, Annie is also accusing Felix of the crime. I would imagine that you came up with a similar answer. We can make these layers of meaning explicit by providing separate paraphrases for the semantic meaning (a semantic paraphrase or SP) and the pragmatic meaning (a pragmatic paraphrase or PP):

> Cats drink cream
> SP: Domestic felines consume the liquid fat of milk.
> PP: Felix probably drank the cream.

Did you notice that when we are talking about what a particular speaker means, our paraphrases can be rather different from the literal meaning of the sentence that was uttered?

Sentence
Utterance

Linguists often make the distinction between a SENTENCE and an UTTERANCE. This distinction can be useful for two reasons. First, pragmatics analyses language in use and many of the utterances we use do not consist of full sentences yet are entirely understandable in context:

> Jane: Coffee?
> Steve: Sure!
> Jane: White?
> Steve: Black.

Second, while we can talk about the two sentences *Cats drink cream* and *Cats drink cream* as being exactly the same, we cannot really say this about utterances because each utterance is a unique event created at a particular point in time for a particular purpose. The next two exercises will illustrate this.

EXERCISE ✎

1.5   Provide a semantic meaning (SP) and a pragmatic meaning (PP) for It's cold in here in two different contexts, (a) and (b) below:

  (a) Mike and Annie are in the living room. Mike asks Annie whether she'd like to eat dinner in the living room or the kitchen. Annie replies: It's cold in here.
  (b) The Queen and her butler, James, are in the drawing room. The window is open. The Queen says: It's cold in here.

Comment

Here are sample analyses.

  (a) It's cold in here
       SP: The temperature in this place is frigid.
       PP: Let's eat in the kitchen
  (b) It's cold in here
       SP: The temperature in this place is frigid.
       PP: James, shut the window.

EXERCISE ✎

1.6   Now provide a third context for It's cold in here which would yield a third and different pragmatic meaning.

Here is one possibility:

Mike and Annie are in the greenhouse. Mike wonders why his orchids haven't bloomed. Annie replies: It's cold in here.

> It's cold in here
> SP: The temperature in this place is frigid.
> PP: The orchids aren't blooming because the greenhouse is too cold.

As you can see, two or more utterances might have the same underlying sentence as their 'script', but they can have quite different interpretations in context. By now you will have noticed that interpreting what a speaker's utterance means involves a fair amount of intelligent guesswork for the hearer, and considerably more knowledge than comes from simply knowing the meanings of individual words and how they combine to form sentences. In the following units, we will be looking in more detail at what this sort of intelligent guesswork might involve.

SUMMARY

- Language meaning can be analysed at several levels.
- Semantics concentrates on the meaning that comes from linguistic knowledge, while pragmatics concentrates on those aspects of meaning that cannot be predicted by linguistic knowledge alone and takes into account our knowledge about the physical and social world.
- The focus of pragmatic analysis is on the meaning of speakers' utterances rather than on the meaning of words or sentences.
- Utterances need not consist of complete sentences. Each utterance is a unique physical event created at a particular point in time for a particular communicative purpose.

✐ FURTHER EXERCISES

1.7 Below are several conversational extracts where the participants are discussing meaning. For each extract decide if the meaning type under discussion would be primarily the concern of semantics or pragmatics.

(a) Mike: That's an interesting hat.
     Annie: What do you mean by that?
(b) Steve: Listen to this. 'No animal bird or reptile shall be kept in the Flat or any other part of the building without the prior written consent of the Lessor which (if given) shall be deemed to be by way of licence revocable at will.'
     Jane: That just means tenants can't have pets without the landlord's written permission and that even if he does give permission, he can take it back any time he wants to.

    (c) Parent: Where are your shoes, young man?
          Child: Under my bed.
          Parent: When I asked where your shoes were, I wanted you to put them on!
    (d) Ed: Lugubrious?
          Faye: You know, sort of mournful, not very cheerful.
    (e) Dave: What did Macbeth mean when he said that life was a tale told by an idiot?
          Sarah: I guess he thought that life didn't make any sense.

1.8   Provide at least one possible semantic paraphrase (SP) for sentences (a)–(d) below.

   Example: *The party is going to begin after he leaves.*

     SP: The party will commence after he departs.

Analyse your paraphrases in terms of whether you changed individual words, the sentence structure, or both.

    (a)   *Her mother is unhappy.*
    (b)   *My friend loathes string beans.*
    (c)   *I'll look for that book right now.*
    (d)   *Steve hugged Jane.*

SUPPLEMEN-
TARY
EXERCISES ✎

1.9   Words can have more than one semantic meaning and consequently so can the sentences in which they appear. For example, *We liked the ball* could have two different semantic meanings:

   SP1:   We liked the sphere.
   SP2:   We liked the dance.

We often have to use our knowledge of the context to predict which one is intended by the speaker, and sometimes we have to 'backtrack'. I saw this sign in the window of a seafood restaurant in the USA:

   We serve shrimps and crabs
   And tall people and nice people too

Provide three **different** semantic meanings (SPs) for the first line of the sign and choose the one that was intended given the second line. Which of the three was your first prediction as you were reading the sign? Can you think of any reasons why that was your first prediction? Did any of them involve your expectations about the world and the way people behave?

1.10   Provide three different contexts in which the utterance I'm hot would have three different pragmatic meanings even though the underlying semantic meaning would remain the same. (Follow the format we used in **Exercise 1.6.**)

1.11   Here is an example of a context where three different utterances could potentially have similar pragmatic meanings, even though each of them has a different semantic meaning. A mother walks into a very messy room and addresses teenage inhabitant:

> This room is a pig sty! How many times have I told you about this room? Clean this room up.

For (a)–(c) below, provide three alternatives for the underlined utterance. Each alternative should potentially have a similar pragmatic meaning, even though the semantic meaning would be different.

(a)   Matt: Do you want some cake?
        Chris: I'm on a diet.
(b)   Ed: How was the party?
        Faye: Don't ask!
(c)   Matt: Lend me a pen.
        Chris: Here. But it's running out of ink.

<svg-like> DISCUSSION QUESTIONS

1.12   Below are four definitions of *pragmatics*. What elements do they have in common? Do you notice any differences in emphasis?

(a)   Pragmatics studies the factors that govern our choice of language in social interaction and the effects of our choice on others.

> (Crystal, 1987, p. 120)

(b)   Pragmatics can be usefully defined as the study of how utterances have meanings in situations.

> (Leech, 1983, p. x)

(c)   Pragmatics is the study of how more gets communicated than is said.

> (Yule, 1996, p. 3)

(d)   There is a distinction between a hearer's knowledge of her language and her knowledge of the world. In this section, I shall argue that it is this distinction that underlies the distinction between semantics and pragmatics.

> (Blakemore, 1992, p. 39)

1.13   Growing up is hard to do! Analyse the semantic and/or pragmatic difficulties these young people have got themselves into. (Examples·(c)–(e) are from American high school students who were asked to define a word and use it in a sentence.)

(a)   A pupil was asked to comment on the line *The child is the father to the man* and answered: This was written by Shakespeare. He often made this kind of mistake.

(b)   Child: Mommy, I want more milk.
 Parent: Is that the way to ask?
 Child: Please.
 Parent: Please what?
 Child: Please gimme milk.

(c)   *Word*   *Student's definition*   *Student's sentence*
 risqué   'daring'   The risqué little squirrel wasn't afraid of the dog.

(d)   *Word*   *Student's definition*   *Student's sentence*
 indefatigable 'tireless'   The Halloween gang left several cars indefatigable.

(e)   *Word*   *Student's definition*   *Student's sentence*
 spurious   'wearing spurs'   The cowboy strode spuriously through the admiring crowd.

FURTHER READING

For short, beginner-level overviews of the types of questions that pragmatics deals with and the relationship between semantics and pragmatics:

Crystal, 1987, pp. 120–22.
Yule, 1996, pp. 3–8.

For more advanced treatment of these issues:

Blakemore, 1992, pp. 39–53.
Leech, 1983, pp. 1–18.

The examples of American high school students wrestling with vocabulary questions come from:

Greene, 1969.

ENTAILMENT

2

In the first unit we saw that interpreting utterances involves a considerable amount of intelligent guesswork where the hearer draws inferences from the speaker's words to arrive at the speaker's meaning. In this unit we look at entailment, a relationship between sentences that forms the basis for some of these inferences.

Exam Question: Draw inferences from the fact that when water freezes, a pipe bursts.
Student's Answer: I have never seen an inference so I cannot draw one.

(From *Howlers* by Russell Ash, 1985)

✎ **EXERCISE**

2.1 Look at the following 'slips' from radio and television announcers. What's wrong here?

(a) It's been an amazing year for Crystal Palace over the past 12 months.
(b) The robbery was committed by a pair of identical twins, both are said to be about age 20.
(c) Send in your competition answers with your name, age, and how old you are.
(d) So you're a housewife and a mother. Do you have any children?

Comment

We normally do not expect people to tell us something we already know. Embedded in every utterance is a considerable amount of 'understood' information which comes from our knowledge of the language itself. The 'slips' in this exercise give or ask for redundant information, information which can be automatically inferred from the meanings of words the speaker has already used. If you know the meaning of *year*, *twins*, *age* and *mother*, then you also know that: a year is 12 months long; twins are the same age; your age is how old you are; a mother has a least one child.

EXERCISE

2.2   Pretend that you have just arrived from another planet. You have learned the vocabulary and grammar of English, but you have never visited Earth before, nor have you ever met or spoken to another Earthling. As is the custom on your planet, you interpret everything you hear literally. Your job is to decide whether each of my following statements is true or false and why.

(a)   My mother is a woman.
(b)   My mother is a doctor.
(c)   The tiger is unhappy.
(d)   The tiger is an animal.
(e)   My mother is a boy.
(f)   The tiger is a reptile.

Comment

Without knowing anything about my mother or the tiger in question, you can quite easily answer 'true' to (a) and (d) because of your knowledge of English. These sentences are necessarily true because of the meaning relationship between the words *mother* and *woman* and between *tiger* and *animal*. These types of sentences are some-

Analytic sentences

times referred to as ANALYTIC SENTENCES. Similarly, given that you interpret everything literally, you can easily answer 'false' to (e) and (f). The meanings of *mother* and *boy* and *tiger* and *reptile* make such

Contradictions

sentences necessarily false, or CONTRADICTIONS. However, (b) and (c) present you with a problem. They may or may not be true. You cannot verify the truth or falsity of those statements by looking in your dictionary. You would need other, non-linguistic, information about my mother and the particular tiger I am referring to. These

Synthetic sentences

are sometimes referred to as SYNTHETIC SENTENCES. If it turns out that my mother actually is a doctor or that the tiger is unhappy, we

Synthetically true

would say that these statements are SYNTHETICALLY TRUE. That is, their truth is based on what is happening in the world, not on what is happening in the language. Similarly, if my mother is an engineer rather than a doctor and the tiger is quite happy, we would say that

Synthetically false

these statements are SYNTHETICALLY FALSE.

2.3 Assume that sentence (a) in each pair is synthetically true. Then look at sentence (b) and decide if you can assume that it is automatically true given the truth of (a).

> 1(a) *Annie caught a trout.*
> 1(b) *Annie caught a fish.*
>
> 2(a) *Annie is thin.*
> 2(b) *Annie is not fat.*
>
> 3(a) *Annie baked a cake.*
> 3(b) *Annie baked something.*

Comment

The answer is 'yes' in all three cases. Once we establish the truth of sentence (a), sentence (b) becomes automatically true because of the meaning relationships between *trout/fish, thin/fat,* and *cake/something.* In each case, we can say that sentence (b) is an ENTAILMENT of sentence (a). All sentences have a number of entailments. That is, other sentences which are automatically true if the original sentence is true. The thing about entailment is that this kind of inference is 'for free'. It requires only a knowledge of the semantic system of the language being used. At this point, you may be wondering whether a PARAPHRASE is the same thing as an entailment. In semantics, a paraphrase is a special kind of entailment. The next exercise will show you what I mean.

Entailment

Paraphrase

2.4 For each pair, decide whether you can assume that sentence (b) is automatically true given the synthetic truth of sentence (a). Then reverse the process. If sentence (b) is synthetically true, can you assume that sentence (a) is automatically true?

> 1(a) *Goldilocks saw a bear.*
> 1(b) *Goldilocks saw an animal.*
>
> 2(a) *This porridge is too cold.*
> 2(b) *This porridge is not too hot.*
>
> 3(a) *Baby Bear cried.*
> 3(b) *Baby Bear wept.*
>
> 4(a) *Mama Bear is in front of Papa Bear.*
> 4(b) *Papa Bear is behind Mama Bear.*

Comment

As you can see, things get a bit more complicated when we look to see if the entailment works both ways. In sentence pairs **1** and **2**, the entailment works in only one direction. If Goldilocks saw a *bear*, then she necessarily saw an *animal*. But if she saw an animal, she could have seen a bear but not necessarily. It could have been a big bad wolf, for example. If something is too *cold*, by definition it cannot be too *hot*. But if the porridge is not too hot, is it necessarily too cold? No. Like Baby Bear's porridge, it could be just right. When there is only ONE-WAY ENTAILMENT, the sentences are not true paraphrases of each other. Sentence pairs **3** and **4** behave somewhat differently. Because of the meaning relationship between *cried/wept* and *in front of/behind*, we have a situation of TWO-WAY or MUTUAL ENTAILMENT between the sentences in each pair. These sentences are paraphrases of each other. The term paraphrase is used in semantics when there is a relationship of mutual entailment between two sentences. Generally speaking, 'entailment', 'analytic sentence' and 'contradiction' are considered to be purely semantic concepts, having to do with sentence meaning rather than speaker meaning. However, these issues can be quite relevant to the study of pragmatics as the next two exercises will illustrate.

One-way entailment

Two-way entailment
Mutual entailment

EXERCISE

2.5   In each of the following dialogues, spot the information which appears redundant or contradictory from a semantic point of view. Then decide in pragmatic terms what this sort of information might be 'telling' the hearer.

(a) Tom: What's your stepmother like?
    Bob: Well, she's a woman and she married my father.

(b) Dave: There's your Uncle George.
    Lucy: That man's a snake.

(c) Jane: You ate all the cookies!
    Steve: I ate some of the cookies.

Comment

In (a) Bob appears to be providing redundant information since his stepmother is necessarily a woman who married his father, given the meaning of *stepmother*. But is this kind of information always useless? Did you get the impression that Bob might not be particularly fond of his stepmother or that perhaps he has not met her yet? In (b) Lucy is providing an inherent contradiction. Semantically, a man is not a snake. However, from a pragmatic point of view, her answer makes a lot of sense. We can infer that she doesn't like her uncle. Dialogue (c) is tricky. Did you assume that Steve had not eaten all the cookies? Did he specifically say that he had not eaten all the cookies? From a purely logical point of view, if Steve ate all the cookies, then he also ate some of them on his way to eating all of them. (The meaning relation between *all/some* is similar to that between *trout/fish* in **Exercise 2.3** and *bear/animal* in **Exercise 2.4**.) If Steve had eaten all the cookies, from a semantic point of view he was not lying. From a pragmatic point of view, well, what do you think? We will be returning to these issues in **Units 4** and **5**.

Take the sentence, *The painters broke the window*. This sentence has many entailments Here are some very basic (one-way) entailments:

Entailment 1:	'Someone broke the window.'
Entailment 2:	'The painters did something to the window.'
Entailment 3:	'The painters broke something.'

When uttering this sentence in context, a speaker will have one of these entailments in mind as the main focus, the most important one for interpreting the message. One way of communicating this to the hearer, or FOREGROUNDING a particular entailment, is by putting heavy stress one of the words in an utterance. For example, by saying The PAINTERS broke the window, the speaker foregrounds **Entailment 1**. The sentence uttered in this particular way generally communicates the message: 'You and I are taking it for granted that someone broke the window. I'm telling you who did it.'

Foregrounding

────────────────────────────

✎ **EXERCISE**

2.6 Here are three different stress patterns for *Annie ruined the sweater*. Try matching each utterance with the entailment which is being foregrounded. While you are doing this, think how the message subtly changes with each change of stress.

Utterance (a):	Annie RUINED the sweater.
Utterance (b):	Annie ruined the SWEATER.
Utterance (c):	ANNIE ruined the sweater.
Entailment 1:	'Someone ruined the sweater.'
Entailment 2:	'Annie did something to the sweater.'
Entailment 3:	'Annie ruined something.'

────────────────────────────

Is your analysis similar to mine?

Comment

Utterance (a) has foregrounded **Entailment 2**. Message: 'You and I are taking it for granted that Annie did something to the sweater. I'm telling you what Annie did.'

Utterance (b) has foregrounded **Entailment 3**. Message: 'You and I are taking it for granted that Annie ruined something. I'm telling you what Annie ruined.'

Utterance (c) has foregrounded **Entailment 1**. Message: 'You and I are taking it for granted that someone ruined the sweater. I'm telling you that Annie did it.'

Each of these different messages illustrates how more can be communicated than simply 'what is said'. The importance given to one entailment over another by a speaker has important consequences for the pragmatic analysis of that utterance.

SUMMARY

- All sentences have a number of entailments – other sentences which are automatically true if the original sentence is true.
- Entailments are inferences that can be drawn solely from our knowledge about the semantic relationships in a language.
- This knowledge allows us to communicate much more than we actually 'say'.

FURTHER EXERCISES ✎

2.7 Which of the following sentences cannot be designated as 'true' or 'false' unless you have extra non-linguistic information?

(a) *My hamster is a mammal.*
(b) *My cousin is a girl.*
(c) *My sister is a girl.*
(d) *My sister is female.*
(e) *I saw a female rock.*
(f) *I saw a female tortoise.*
(g) *My cat likes ice-cream.*
(h) *My sick cat is not well.*

2.8   For each sentence (a)–(d) provide two entailments. One should be a one-way entailment as in these examples:

Ed caught a trout → Ed caught a fish
Original sentence   Entailment
The blimp was over the house → Something was over the house
Original sentence   Entailment

and one should be a two-way (mutual) entailment as in these examples:

Ed caught a trout ↔ Ed captured a trout
Original sentence   Entailment
The blimp was over the house ↔ The house was under the blimp
Original sentence   Entailment

Use → to show one-way entailment and ↔ to show two-way entailment. Every sentence has many possible entailments, but remember, in semantics an entailment must be automatically true solely by virtue of meaning relationships in the language, not by virtue of what usually happens in the world. For example, *Jane is intelligent* entails *Jane is not stupid* but does **not** entail *Jane does well at university* or even *Jane is a woman*. (Jane could be a baby, or a pet hamster or a man with an unusual name. You need more than purely linguistic knowledge to say that 'she' is a woman.)

(a) *My sister-in-law grows roses.*
(b) *Steve is furious.*
(c) *Tom sold a computer to Mark.*
(d) *My brother repaired my car.*

✐ **SUPPLE-
MENTARY
EXERCISES**

2.9 Write three analytic sentences, e.g. *My mother is a woman.* For each sentence, think of a context where the utterance of that apparently 'uninformative' sentence would be quite informative to the hearer.

2.10 Write three sentences which are contradictions, e.g. *My mother is a boy.* For each sentence, think of a context where the utterance of that apparently 'nonsensical' sentence would still make sense to the hearer.

2.11 The following are from *Howlers* by Russell Ash (1985) and *The 776 Stupidest Things Ever Said* by Ross and Kathryn Petras (1994). Where has the communication gone wrong? Or has it?

(a) All creatures are imperfect beasts. Man alone is the perfect beast.
(b) The brain of a woman is almost as heavy as a human brain.
(c) A coroner's duty is to decide whether a person died a fatal death.
(d) We do not have censorship. What we have is a limitation on what newspapers can report.
(e) Snakes are two sexes, poisonous and non-poisonous.
(f) I have reiterated over and over again what I have said before.

💬 **DISCUSSION
QUESTIONS**

2.12 Look at these pairs of utterances. The sentences being uttered in each pair are arguably semantic paraphrases of each other (in a relationship of mutual entailment). Do you think they communicate the same information?

1(a) That food was delicious.
1(b) That grub was yummy.

2(a) She designs clothes for adult male humans.
2(b) She designs clothes for men.

3(a) That guy's a bachelor.
3(b) That guy never got married.

2.13   In **Exercise 2.6** we noticed that heavy stress on a word can be used to foreground a particular entailment. Certain kinds of sentence structure can also do this and are particularly useful in written language where stress is not available. The second sentence here is called a CLEFT SENTENCE:

Cleft sentence

(a) The PAINTERS broke the window. (spoken)
(b) It was the painters who broke the window. (written)

When the cleft construction is used in spoken language combined with heavy stress, some interesting meaning differences can emerge. Compare:

(c) It wasn't ME who burnt the toast.
(d) It WASN'T me who burnt the toast.

2.14   '... the entailments of a sentence can be regarded as those propositions that can be inferred from it <u>in any context</u>' (my underlining, Simpson, 1993: 122). What problems, if any, are posed for this definition by a sentence like *George saw a nut*?

FURTHER READING

For more about the role of entailment in pragmatic analysis:

Yule, 1996, Chapter 4.
Simpson, 1993, Chapter 5.

For more about different meaning relationships between words and different types of entailment:

Hurford and Heasley, 1988, Units 9–11.

PRESUPPOSITION

3

> We look at presupposition, another kind of inference which is very closely linked to the 'working' of the utterance.

> I celebrate myself and sing myself,
> And what I assume, you shall assume.
> (Walt Whitman)

In the USA, an accused mugger rather foolishly chose to defend himself at the trial. The following is one of the questions he put to his victim:

> Did you get a good look at my face when I took your purse?

This goes some way to explaining why he was sentenced to 10 years in prison, but it also highlights another type of inference that we make when interpreting utterances. In the previous unit we experimented with assigning 'true' or 'false' to sentences. For some sentences, like *My mother is a woman*, we could assign a TRUTH-VALUE based on what was happening in the language. For others, like *My mother is a doctor*, we could still assign a truth-value, but it had to be based on what was happening in the world.

Truth-value

✎ **EXERCISE**

3.1 Decide if it is possible to assign either 'true' or false' to each of the following sentences. (Remember, 'true' and 'false' are not quite the same as 'yes' and 'no'.) Are there any sentences where this was not quite possible regardless of how much knowledge you had about the people, places and events involved or the meaning of English words?

17

> (a) *Abraham Lincoln is the current president of the USA.*
> (b) *The Eiffel Tower is in Paris.*
> (c) *A car is an automobile.*
> (d) *Have a cookie.*
> (e) *Be careful of the crumbs.*
> (f) *Where was Abraham Lincoln born?*
> (g) *How much did the car cost?*

Comment

You could answer 'false' to (a) and 'true' to (b) based on your knowledge about the world. You could automatically answer 'true' to (c) based on your knowledge of what *car* and *automobile* mean. These three sentences have a particular kind of grammatical structure. They

**Declarative
sentences**

are DECLARATIVE SENTENCES. Declarative sentences typically function as 'statements'.

> *You   ran   away.*
> | |
> Subject   Verb

Problems in assigning 'true' or 'false' occur in sentences (d) to (g) These sentences do not have a declarative structure. Sentences (d)

**Imperative
sentences**

and (e) are IMPERATIVE SENTENCES. In imperative sentences, which typically function as 'commands', there is no subject present although it is 'understood' as *you*.

> *Run   away!*
> |
> Verb

**Interrogative
sentences**

Sentences (f) and (g) are INTERROGATIVE SENTENCES. Interrogative sentences typically function as 'questions'. Some interrogatives begin with words like *who, what, when ,where, why, how*, etc. Since the majority of these words begin with *wh-*, they are all usually called

Wh-words

WH-WORDS.

> *Why did   you   run away?   Did   you   run away?*
> | | | | | |
> Verb Subject Verb   Verb Subject Verb

You will recall from **Unit 2** that the entailments of a sentence are other sentences which are automatically true if the original sentence is true. However, as we have seen, only declarative sentences can be 'true' or 'false'. Does this mean what we cannot draw some very strong inferences from utterances based on imperative and interrogative sentences?

3.2 For each of the following utterances decide whether the sentence being uttered is declarative, imperative or interrogative and whether the accompanying inference seems valid.

(a) Where has Faye looked for the keys? 'Faye has looked for the keys.'
(b) Did you buy this awful wine? 'This wine is awful.'
(c) Don't sit on Annie's sofa. 'Annie has a sofa.'
(d) Stop being lazy. 'You are being lazy.'
(e) Lucy knows that George is a crook. 'George is a crook'.

Comment

These inferences all seem quite obvious ones to make. They look suspiciously like entailments, yet only the sentence uttered in (e) is declarative. Sentences (a) and (b) are interrogatives, and sentences (c) and (d) are imperatives. These sorts of inferences are sometimes called PRESUPPOSITIONS. Since not all utterances consist of full declarative sentences, presupposition can be a useful concept when analysing speaker meaning. However, it has proved very difficult for authors in the area to agree on a definition for it. This definition problem is partly a reflection of the fuzzy boundary between pragmatics and semantics. Some definitions of presupposition are very broad and speaker oriented: anything the speaker assumes to be true before making the utterance. Others are much more narrow and sentence oriented: a necessary precondition for the sentence to be true. In these units we will be treating presuppositions as inferences about what is assumed to be true in the utterance rather than directly asserted to be true:

Presuppositions

Faye has looked for the keys **directly asserts** 'Faye has looked for the keys'
Where has Faye looked for the keys? **presupposes** 'Faye has looked for the keys'
Annie has a sofa **directly asserts** 'Annie has a sofa'
Don't sit on Annie's sofa **presupposes** 'Annie has a sofa'

Presuppositions are inferences that are very closely linked to the words and grammatical structures actually used in the utterance, but they come from our knowledge about the way language users **conventionally interpret** these words and structures. Because of this, presuppositions can be quite 'sneaky' as the next exercise will demonstrate.

EXERCISE

3.3 In **Exercise 3.2** change *has* to *hasn't* in (a); *did* to *didn't* in (b); *do* to *don't* in (c); *stop* to *don't stop* in (d); and *knows* to *doesn't know* in (e). Do the inferences still hold?

Comment

Negation

You will have found that each of these inferences, or presuppositions, remains constant under NEGATION of the main sentence. (Unfortunately for our mugger at the beginning of the unit, the inference that he took the purse would still hold whether or not his victim said she got a good look at his face.) This is sometimes used as a 'test' for a presupposition, and it highlights how a presupposition can take on the appearance of 'established truth'. In the next three exercises, we will look in a bit more detail at some of the kinds of words and structures that seem to 'trigger' presuppositions.

EXERCISE

3.4 Each of the following utterances mentions *chocolate cake*. Decide which ones contain the presupposition that at the time the utterance was made 'There **was** a chocolate cake'. What do those utterances have in common?

1(a) Mike might find the chocolate cake in the kitchen.
1(b) Mike might find a chocolate cake in the kitchen.

2(a) Is Mike giving Annie that chocolate cake?
2(b) Is Mike giving Annie a chocolate cake?

3(a) Did Mike hide a chocolate cake?
3(b) Did Mike hide Annie's chocolate cake?

Comment

Possessives

Definite noun phrase

The (a) utterance in each pair leads us to presuppose that the chocolate cake being mentioned actually existed. What we notice is that in each of those utterances the noun *cake* is part of a larger noun phrase. The words *the, that, this, these, those*, and POSSESSIVES like *Annie's, my, your*, etc. make it a DEFINITE NOUN PHRASE and trigger this very basic kind of presupposition. Notice that possessives lead to a particularly strong presupposition about the existence of the chocolate cake, and in addition lead to the presupposition that 'Annie has a chocolate cake'. This basic type of presupposition is

Existential presupposition

sometimes called an EXISTENTIAL PRESUPPOSITION. Look at how existential presupposition could work if I wanted to sell you some hair lotion:

You'll want DomeBeGone, my revolutionary cure for baldness.

Here, I am directly asserting that 'You will want it' but inside the definite noun phrase *my revolutionary cure for baldness* lurk several quite dubious propositions which are simply assumed to be true:

'There is a cure for baldness.'
'The cure is revolutionary.'
'I have this cure.'

You can probably see that presupposition has a great deal of importance in persuasive language, particularly in the courtroom and in advertising. Advertisers are not allowed to directly assert claims about their products or their competitors' for which they have no evidence. However, they can generally get away with making indirect assertions via presupposition. In the courtroom, where the stakes are much higher than in advertising, lawyers examining witnesses are often not allowed to make an indirect assertion via presupposition, unless it has been established by previous evidence.

✎ **EXERCISE**

3.5 For each of the following utterances, decide which ones contain the presupposition that 'Mike smashed the television'. In other words, which ones indicate that the speaker has assumed that this proposition is true but has not directly asserted it. What do those utterances have in common?

(a) Did Mike smash the television?
(b) When did Mike smash the television?
(c) I was eating popcorn when Mike smashed the television.
(d) Why did Mike smash the television?
(e) I don't understand why Mike smashed the television.
(f) I wonder if Mike smashed the television.
(g) I wonder how Mike smashed the television.

Comment

Here (b), (c), (d), (e), and (g) seem to presuppose that Mike smashed the television, while (a) and (f) leave it as an 'open question'. Wh-words like *when, why, how*, etc. can trigger suppositions both when they are used to ask a question as in (b) and (d) and when they introduce a SUBORDINATE CLAUSE as in (c), (e), and (g): *when/why/ how Mike smashed the television.*

Subordinate clause

✎ **EXERCISE**

3.6 In this exercise we look at some other kinds of words and constructions that can lead to presuppositions. In each case write out a presupposition contained in the utterance and decide what has triggered it.

> (a) Steve regrets buying a dog.
> (b) Meridyth pretends she's a rock star.
> (c) Ed should stop eating raw oysters.

Comment

Mine were: (a) 'Steve bought a dog'. (b) 'Meridyth is not a rock star'. (c) 'Ed eats raw oysters'. Interestingly, when hearers query presuppositions, they often explicitly query the wording that leads to them as well:

> Steve could hardly <u>regret</u> it since he didn't buy the dog after all.
> <u>Pretend</u>? I thought Meridyth WAS a rock star.
> What do you mean '<u>stop</u>'? Ed's never eaten a raw oyster in his life!

The use of *regret* in (a) triggers the presupposition that what follows is 'fact'. Other verbs that can behave like this are *know*, *realize*, *discover* and *find out* as well as constructions like *I'm aware that . . .* and *It's strange that . . .* On the other hand, the use of *pretend* in (b) triggers the presupposition that what follows is 'fiction'. Other verbs that can behave like this are *imagine* and *dream* and constructions like *If I were . . .* as in *If I were the Prime Minister, I'd ban presuppositions.* The use of *stop* in (c) triggers the presupposition that the action was going on before. Other verbs that can behave like this are *continue* and *keep*. On the other hand, *start* and *begin* can presuppose that the action was **not** going on before.

In this unit we have been looking at utterances in isolation, as if we had just passed by an open door and overheard a stranger talking. Presuppositions seem to be inferences that can be made with very little knowledge of the context. In the next unit we will start looking at inferences that require considerably more contextual knowledge and possibly more work for the hearer as well.

SUMMARY

- We have described presuppositions as inferences about what is assumed in an utterance rather than directly asserted.
- Presuppositions are closely linked to the words and grammatical structures that are actually used in the utterance and our knowledge about the way language users conventionally interpret them.
- Presuppositions can be drawn even when there is little or no surrounding context.

3.7   In each case assume that the judge has sustained an objection to the question. What presupposition(s) might have been objected to?

    (a) How did you know that the defendant had bought a knife?

    (b) How long have you been selling cocaine?

    (c) When was your bracelet stolen?

    (d) Did you see the murdered woman before she left the office?

    (e) How fast was the car going when the driver ran the red light?

    (f) At what time did you telephone your lover?

    (g) Have you stopped being an active gang member?

    (h) Why did you leave the scene of the crime?

3.8   In each of the following advertisement extracts, what claim or claims are being made by presupposition rather than directly asserted? (The names have been changed to protect the innocent.)

    (a) The secret to Blasee's effectiveness is Calming Fluid.

    (b) Look out for the distinctive packs in your local Bippo stockists and choose the one that's just right for you.

    (c) Watch all the puffiness and wrinkles disappear!

    (d) Increased protection against water spots.

    (e) Now you can get a really crisp professional finish.

    (f) It combines three potent skin perfecting discoveries in one gentle formula.

3.9   Try your hand at being a tricky lawyer. Write some questions that attempt to sneak in the following 'facts' via presupposition. Here's a sample question for 'The defendant drove his car into a shop window': **Did you brake before you drove your car into the shop window?** Notice how if the defendant 'just answers the question', either **Yes** or **No**, he accepts the truth of the presupposition and admits that he drove his car into the shop window.

    (a) The defendant had a fight with his brother-in-law.

    (b) The defendant has three previous convictions.

    (c) The defendant belongs to a terrorist organization.

    (d) The defendant was speeding.

3.10   Try your hand at being a tricky advertiser. Below are completely unsubstantiated claims about various products. For each one, write a line of advertisement that slips in the claim via presupposition. For the purposes of this exercise use full sentences. Your sentences can be declaratives, interrogatives or imperatives. In fact, you will find interrogatives and imperatives particularly useful in some cases.

(a)   ZONKO cures insomnia.
(b)   HappyHavens Inn has beautiful views.
(c)   KISSGOOD eliminates bad breath.
(d)   NO-ANT kills ants.
(e)   Crook & Sons Ltd employ skilled workers.
(f)   BLASTEX is not poisonous.
(g)   SHINO nourishes wood.
(h)   Dogs love YAPPY dog food.
(i)   Dentists use GRIN toothpaste.

DISCUSSION QUESTIONS

3.11   Since we have said that presuppositions arise from conventional interpretations, could we extend this to *and*? Here are some utterances to play with:

(a)   It was hot and very humid.
(b)   Ed ate the raw oysters and felt quite ill.
(c)   Ed got dressed and went to the office.

3.12   Would you consider it unusual for a hearer to query an entailment?

3.13   Do all of these utterances presuppose 'The boiler blew up'?

(a)   John got to safety before the boiler blew up.
(b)   John got to the safety valve before the boiler blew up.
(c)   John got to safety after the boiler blew up.
(d)   John got to the safety valve after the boiler blew up.

FURTHER READING

For an interesting discussion of how presupposition fits into semantics and pragmatics:

Simpson, 1993, Chapter 5.

For more about the case of the exploding boiler:

Yule, 1996, pp. 99–100.

For a review of the problems in defining presupposition:

Leech, 1981, Chapter 14.

THE CO-OPERATIVE PRINCIPLE AND IMPLICATURE

4

We look at a third type of inferencing, implicature, and at how speakers co-operate in a conversation to achieve a shared meaning for utterances.

Don't quote what he says. Say what he means!
(Senator Barry Goldwater's campaign aide to reporters)

✏ **EXERCISE**

4.1 What might the second speaker 'mean' in each of the following dialogues? Write a pragmatic paraphrase in each case, and think about how you inferred this meaning.

(a) Virginia: Do you like my new hat?
    Mary: It's pink!

(b) Maggie: Coffee?
    James: It would keep me awake all night.

(c) Linda: Have you finished the student evaluation forms and the reading lists?
    Jean: I've done the reading lists.

(d) Phil: Are you going to Steve's barbecue?
    Terry: Well, Steve's got those dogs now.

(e) Annie: Was the dessert any good?
    Mike: Annie, cherry pie is cherry pie.

Comment

Here are some possible paraphrases:

(a) 'I don't like your hat.'
(b) 'I won't have some coffee.'
(c) 'I haven't done the evaluation forms.'
(d) 'I don't think I'm going to Steve's barbecue.'
(e) 'No, the dessert was pretty boring.'

There appear to be many ways of saying 'No'. Yet *no* or *not* did not appear in any of the original responses. You may have also found that you drew a somewhat different inference for some of these utterances. For example, not everyone infers that the speaker in (a) does not like the hat or that the speaker in (e) was not very keen on the dessert. These kinds of inferences or CONVERSATIONAL IMPLICATURES, to use their technical term, seem to be less 'straightforward' than those based on entailment or presupposition.

Conversational implicatures

EXERCISE ✎

4.2   Let's look at Mary's, James's, Jean's, Terry's and Mike's responses in **Exercise 4.1** – this time, with a different utterance from the first speaker. The content of the second speaker's utterance remains the same, but does the meaning remain the same? Write a pragmatic paraphrase for the second speaker's response in each dialogue.

(a) Virginia: Try the roast pork.
    Mary: It's pink!

(b) Maggie: We went to see *The Omen* last night but it wasn't very scary.
    James: It would keep me awake all night.

(c) Linda: You look very pleased with yourself.
    Jean: I've done the reading lists.

(d) Phil: His garden looks awful.
    Terry: Well, Steve's got those dogs now.

(e) Annie: I thought the pie would cheer you up.
    Mike: Annie, cherry pie is cherry pie.

Comment

Some typical pragmatic paraphrases are:

(a) 'I'm not having the roast pork.'
(b) 'I think *The Omen* is scary.'
(c) 'I am pleased with myself, because I've done the reading lists.'
(d) 'Steve's dogs have wrecked the garden.'
(e) 'It takes more than cherry pie to cheer me up.'

As you can see, the context provided by the previous utterance can lead to quite a different implicature in each case.

4.3   Now we return to the **original** dialogues, (a), (b), and (e) in **Exercise 4.1**. How do you think the first speaker would interpret the second speaker's response if you had the following extra information?

- Pink is Mary's favourite colour and Virginia knows this.
- James has to stay up all night to study for an exam and Maggie knows this.
- Mike loves cherry pie. As far as he's concerned, no one can ruin a cherry pie, and Annie knows this.

Comment

Most people would now interpret the responses in (a), (b) and (e) to mean 'yes'. As you can see, drawing the appropriate implicature can require a considerable amount of shared knowledge between the speaker and the hearer.

Just how we achieve this level of meaning was an issue tackled by the philosopher, Paul Grice. Grice proposed that all speakers, regardless of their cultural background, adhere to a basic principle governing conversation which he termed THE CO-OPERATIVE PRIN-CIPLE. That is, we assume that in a conversation the participants will co-operate with each other when making their contributions. Grice then broke this principle down into four basic MAXIMS which go towards making a speaker's contribution to the conversation 'co-operative':

The co-operative principle

Maxims

1   RELEVANCE: Make sure that whatever you say is relevant to the conversation at hand.

Relevance

2   QUALITY: Do not say what you believe to be false. Do not say that for which you lack adequate evidence.

Quality

3   QUANTITY: Make your contribution sufficiently informative for the current purposes of the conversation. Do not make your contribution more informative than is necessary.

Quantity

4   CLARITY: Do not make your contribution obscure, ambiguous or difficult to understand.

Clarity

Grice pointed out that these maxims are not always observed, but he makes a distinction between 'quietly' VIOLATING a maxim and openly FLOUTING a maxim. Violations are 'quiet' in the sense that it is not obvious at the time of the utterance that the speaker has **deliberately** lied, supplied insufficient information, or been ambiguous, irrelevant or hard to understand. In Grice's analysis, these violations might hamper communication but they do not lead to implicatures. What leads to implicatures is a situation where the speaker **flouts** a maxim. That is, it is obvious to the hearer at the time of the utterance that the speaker has deliberately and quite

Violating

Flouting

openly failed to observe one or more maxims. To see how Grice's analysis might work in practice, try the next exercise.

EXERCISE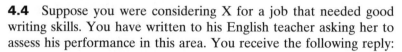

4.4 Suppose you were considering X for a job that needed good writing skills. You have written to his English teacher asking her to assess his performance in this area. You receive the following reply:

'X has regularly and punctually attended all my classes. All his assignments were handed in on time and very neatly presented. I greatly enjoyed having X in my class.'

(a) What maxim does the teacher seem to flout?
(b) What implicature would you draw about X's writing skills?
(c) Why do you think the teacher phrased her response this way?

Comment

(a) The teacher's response appears to flout the maxim of quantity. There is insufficient information about X's writing skills, yet we would assume that as his English teacher, she would have this information. (b) Most people infer that X's writing skills are not very good even though at no point is this explicitly stated. This is a classic example of 'damning with faint praise'. (c) Grice observed that in

Clash

conversations, we are sometimes faced with a CLASH between maxims. Here the teacher knows that she should give an *informative* answer to the question (quantity). She also knows that she should only say what is *truthful* (quality). The teacher does not want to state baldly that the student's performance was not very good. (For example, she might think that X will see the reference letter.) At the same time she does not want to lie. So, she makes her response in such a way that the reader can infer this without her having to state it. According to Grice, the implicature is made possible by the fact that we normally assume that speakers do not really abandon the co-operative principle.

Following Grice's reasoning, the inference is worked out like this:

1 Since I have good reason to believe that she has information about X's writing skills, the speaker has deliberately failed to observe (flouted) the maxim 'Be informative'.
2 But I have no reason to believe that she has really opted out of the co-operative principle. So, she is only being **apparently** uninformative.
3 If I draw the inference that X hasn't got very good writing skills, then the speaker **is** being co-operative. She knows that I am capable of working this out.
4 Therefore, she has implied (or 'implicated' to use Grice's term) that the student's writing skills are not very good.

As you can see, this sort of inferencing occurs in stages. In the first stage, the hearer recognizes the apparent irrelevancy, inadequacy, lack of clarity, etc. This in turn triggers the implicature.

4.5 Speech therapist: So you like ice-cream.
                                      What are your favourite
                                      flavours?
     Child with a pragmatic disorder: Hamburger . . . fish and
                                      chips
                     (Adapted from Bishop, 1997, p. 183)

Which maxim has the child failed to observe? Would you consider this a case of flouting or violation of that maxim?

Comment

The child, who has not realized that *favourite flavours* should be interpreted as 'favourite flavours of ice-cream' rather than 'favourite flavours in general', has failed to observe the maxim of relevance. He generally has difficulty taking the context into account when making his contribution in a conversation. Because his irrelevance is not deliberate, we would view this as a violation rather than a flouting of the maxim. Had I only labelled the speakers 'A' and 'B', would you have interpreted B's utterance as a joke? Humour based on taking liberties with the co-operative principle is a frequent feature in comic writing. The Marx Brothers, for example, are famous for their anarchic approach to conversation.

> (The ship's captain is looking for stowaways, one of whom is Groucho.)
> Groucho: Yeah? What do they look like?
> Captain: One goes around with a black mustache.
> Groucho: Well, you couldn't expect a mustache to go around by itself. Don't you think a mustache ever gets lonely, Captain?
>   (Anobile, 1972, p. 57)

> (Groucho has just become the new head of Huxley College.)
> Professor: My dear Professor, I'm sure the students would appreciate a brief outline of your plans for the future.
> Groucho: What?
> Professor: I said the students would appreciate a brief outline of your plans for the future.
> Groucho: You just said that. That's the trouble around here. Talk, talk, talk! Oh sometimes I think I must go mad. Where will it all end?
>   (Anobile, 1972, p. 101)

SUMMARY

- Unlike presuppositions and entailments, implicatures are inferences that cannot be made from isolated utterances. They are dependent on the context of the utterance and shared knowledge between the speaker and the hearer.
- Grice has proposed a way of analysing implicatures based on the co-operative principle and its maxims of relevance, quality, quantity and clarity.
- In Grice's analysis, the speaker's flouting of a maxim combined with the hearer's assumption that the speaker has not really abandoned the co-operative principle leads to an implicature.

FURTHER EXERCISES ✎

4.6 In each of the following decide whether the inference in brackets is a presupposition or an implicature derived from the underlined utterance.

(a) A: My boyfriend lives in Luton
    B: My boyfriend lives in Paris. (I have a boyfriend)

(b) A: What?
    B: Why are you laughing at me? (You are laughing at me)

(c) A: Why is she eating those?
    B: Her father didn't give her any supper. (She didn't have any supper)

(d) A: Is Mike engaged?
    B: He's bought a ring. (Mike is engaged)

(e) A: You look pleased.
    B: I managed to pass the exam. (I tried to pass the exam)

(f) A: Did you finish that report?
    B: I started it. (I didn't finish the report)

4.7 In each case below decide which maxim has not been observed. Then decide whether this was a case of **flouting** or **violation**. Where you think there has been a case of flouting, what implicature might be drawn? Background information is given in square brackets.

(a) Annie: Mike, did you pass the driving test?
    Mike: No. [Mike knows he's passed the driving test]

(b) Annie: Do you want seconds?
    Mike: gmmm uh mmm [Mike's just had his wisdom teeth extracted]

(c) Annie: I really liked that dinner.
    Mike: I'm a vegetarian.

(d) Teacher: What time is it? [towards the end of a lecture]
    Student: It's 10:44 and 35.6 seconds.

(e) Student A: How are you?
    Student B: I'm dead.

(f) Host: Would you like a cocktail? It's my own invention.
    Guest: Well, mmm uh it's not that we don't not drink.

✎ **SUPPLE-MENTARY EXERCISES**

4.8 Return to **Exercise 4.1**, and decide which maxim was flouted by the second speaker in each dialogue.

4.9 Here are three implicatures: 'I don't like it'; 'Steve hates cats'; 'Ed is lazy'. For each of these implicatures write two different dialogues which could lead to that implicature. Each dialogue should involve the flouting of a different maxim. Here are two examples for the implicature 'I'm not going':

1 A: We're going to the movies.
  B: I've got an exam tomorrow.

Relevance: the speaker's exam in not apparently relevant to a discussion about going to the movies.

2 A: Are you going to Steve's barbecue?
  B: A barbecue is an outdoor party.

Quantity: stating that a barbecue is an outdoor party is apparently both too informative (since people know that a barbecue is an outdoor party) and not informative enough since B has not directly answered the question.

4.10 Speakers often show they are aware of the co-operative principle when they use 'HEDGES' which indicate that they may be violating a maxim. What maxim is being alluded to in each case?

Hedges

(a) I don't mean to change the subject, but there's an enormous wasp in here.
(b) This is a bit convoluted but . . .
(c) Well, I think he's honest.
(d) You probably already know this but . . .

DISCUSSION QUESTIONS

4.11   Why might speakers call attention to the fact that they may be violating a maxim? Think of some other common hedges that are used in this way.

4.12   Gesture, facial expression and tone of voice cannot be recreated on the printed page, and yet a great deal of the communication in a conversation involves these channels. Take the dialogues in **Exercise 4.1** and see if you could make the second speakers' responses imply 'yes' rather than 'no' simply by using particular gestures, facial expressions or tones of voice to accompany the utterance.

4.13   Blakemore (1992) has pointed out that we generally do not assume speakers to be communicating unless we assume they are rational, or in other words, unless we think they are conforming to certain norms and standards. Do you agree? To start you thinking, here are some sample utterances from two schizophrenic patients. (You might also want to include the data from the Marx Brothers in your discussion.)

Doctor: Good morning.
Patient A: A real magnanimous good morning to you on this first Wednesday of our glorious New Year.

Doctor: Where should we send it?
Patient B: Kindly send it to me at the hospital. Send it to me, Joseph Nemo, in care of Joseph Nemo and me who answers to the name of Joseph Nemo will care for it myself.

(Data adapted from Obler and Menn, 1982)

FURTHER READING

For more about Grice's theories:

Grice, 1989 (quite advanced) or Yule, 1996, pp. 100–1 for a short extract from Grice.

For a very interesting discussion of children with pragmatic disorders:

Bishop, 1997, Chapters 7 and 8.

MORE ON IMPLICATURES

5

We look in more detail at different kinds of implicatures and find that some are less dependent on background knowledge of the context than others.

> And, after all, what is a lie?
> 'Tis but the truth in masquerade.
>   (Byron, *Don Juan*)

✎ EXERCISE

5.1 For each dialogue, answer the accompanying question based on the implicature that you can draw from the second speaker's response. Think about why you drew those implicatures.

   (a) Carmen: Did you get the milk and the eggs?
       Dave: I got the milk.
       Did Dave buy the eggs?

   (b) Carmen: Did you manage to fix that leak?
       Dave: I tried to.
       Did Dave fix the leak?

   (c) Faye: I hear you've invited Mat and Chris.
       Ed: I didn't invite Mat.
       Did Ed invite Chris?

   (d) Steve: What happened to your flowers?
       Jane: A dog got into the garden.
       Did the dog belong to Jane?

Comment

Most people would draw the implicatures:

(a) 'Dave did not buy the eggs.'
(b) 'Dave did not fix the leak.'
(c) 'Ed invited Chris.'
(d) 'The dog did not belong to Jane.'

These implicatures are based on the quantity of information offered by the speaker. In (a) and (c) we notice that the first speaker's utterance contains *and*. In (a) Carmen is really asking two questions: *Did you buy the milk?* and *Did you buy the eggs?* Similarly, in (c) Faye mentions two propositions: *You invited Mat* and *You invited Chris.* When only one of the questions or propositions has been mentioned in the response, we normally assume that the speaker is still adhering to the co-operative principle and therefore is implying a response for the second one as well. And, we normally take it to be the opposite of the one mentioned. If Dave had bought the eggs as well, he would have said so. If Ed had not invited Chris as well, he would have said so. In (b) the implicature comes from the word *try*. Trying to fix the leak is an intermediate step to managing to fix the leak. The fact that Dave only mentioned the intermediate step leads us to infer that he did not make it to the final step. The implicature in (d) is based on the use of the INDEFINITE ARTICLE *a/an*. We infer that if the dog had belonged to Jane, she would have referred to it as *my dog*. In a more general sense, when the speaker uses the expression *a/an X* we draw the implicature 'not the speaker's X'.

Indefinite article

Our expectations about the quantity of information that speakers will provide in an utterance also lead to other common implicatures, as we will see in the next two exercises.

EXERCISE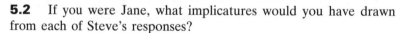

5.2   If you were Jane, what implicatures would you have drawn from each of Steve's responses?

(a) Jane: Who used all the printer paper?
    Steve: I used some of it.

(b) Jane: I hear you're always late with the rent.
    Steve: Well, sometimes I am.

(c) Jane: Mike and Annie should be here by now. Was their plane late?
    Steve: Possibly.

Now look at this dialogue. Would you normally infer that Steve had not kept the cheese in the freezer?

(d) Jane: This cheese looks funny. The label said to store it in a cool place.
    Steve: Yeah, I did.

Most people draw the following implicatures:

(a) 'Steve did not use all of the printer paper, only some of it.'
(b) 'Steve is not always late with the rent, only sometimes.'
(c) 'Steve did not know for certain that the plane was late.'
(d) 'Steve did not freeze the cheese.'

5.3   Now examine those implicatures in light of the following information known only to Steve. Would you say that Steve was lying to Jane in **Exercise 5.2**? Why?

(a) Steve has in fact used all the printer paper.
(b) Steve has been late with the rent every month since he moved in.
(c) Steve knows for a fact that the plane was late because Mike and Annie called him from the airport.
(d) Steve had absentmindedly put the cheese in the freezer and thawed it out before dinner hoping that Jane wouldn't notice.

You will recall from **Unit 2** that from a semantic point of view, because *all* logically entails *some*, Steve's response in (a) is technically true. The same kind of logic applies to (b)–(d) as well. However, from a pragmatic point of view, Steve's utterances have certainly misled Jane because of the implicatures that people normally draw in these circumstances. Steve's trickery involved what we call SCALAR IMPLICATURES. All of Steve's responses use words that participate in a scale of values:

Scale of quantity: ***some***   *most*   *all*
Scale of frequency: ***sometimes***   *often*   *always*
Scale of coldness: ***cool***   *cold*   *freezing*
Scale of likelihood: ***possibly***   *probably*   *certainly*

We normally assume (following the co-operative principle) that, where speakers have a scale of values at their disposal, they will choose the one that is truthful (maxim of quality) and optimally informative (maxim of quantity). So, we normally draw the implicature 'not any of the higher values on the scale'. In other words, if Steve has chosen the word *sometimes*, it creates the implicatures 'not always' and 'not often'. It appears that in each case Steve has technically adhered to the quality maxim but violated quantity. Nevertheless, most of us would think that from a pragmatic point of view Steve was lying since he knew that anybody would draw those inferences.

Have you noticed that while the implicatures we have been looking at require a previous utterance, they are so 'strong' that they do not

Generalized conversational implicatures

seem to require any extra knowledge to extract the meaning? These types of implicatures are sometimes called GENERALIZED CONVERSATIONAL IMPLICATURES.

EXERCISE ✎

5.4 Look at each of these dialogues and the implicatures which appear in brackets. Then decide what knowledge the speaker and hearer would have to share in order for that implicature to be drawn:

(a) Tom: Are you going to Mark's party tonight?
    Annie: My parents are in town. ('No')

(b) Tom: Where's the salad dressing?
    Gabriela: We've run out of olive oil. ('There isn't any salad dressing')

(c) Steve: What's with your mother?
    Jane: Let's go into the garden. ('I can't talk about it in here')

(d) Mat: Want some fudge brownies?
    Chris: There must be 20,000 calories there. ('No')

Comment

For (a) both parties would have to know about Annie's relationship with her parents. For example, if they both knew that Annie tried to avoid her parents at every opportunity, the implication would be 'Yes'. For (b) both parties would have to have some general knowledge – olive oil is a possible ingredient in salad dressing. But both parties also need to share the knowledge that they only use salad dressing made from olive oil. For (c) there would have to be something in the physical context of the utterance to suggest that someone might overhear Jane's answer. For example, if there was no one else present, Steve might well infer that the problem with Jane's mother has something to do with the garden. For (d) both parties again need some general knowledge – food with a high number of calories makes people put on weight. But both parties would also need to share the knowledge that Chris is trying to lose weight. If they both knew that he was trying to gain weight, the implication would be 'Yes'. Inferences which require this kind of shared knowledge between the speaker and hearer are sometimes called PARTICULARIZED CONVERSATIONAL IMPLICATURES.

Particularized conversational implicatures

At this point, you may be wondering about generalized implicatures. They seem so conventional and require so little contextual knowledge that perhaps they are really the same as presuppositions. There is a test that is sometimes used to distinguish presuppositions from implicatures.

5.5 Here are four dialogues where Annie has 'cancelled' either a presupposition contained in her utterance or an implicature that could be drawn from her utterance (the cancellation comes after the 'dash'). Do you notice a difference between presuppositions and implicatures when they are cancelled?

(a) Cancelling an existential presupposition:
Mike: What happened?
Annie: Steve's dog wrecked the garden – and in fact, Steve doesn't have a dog.

(b) Cancelling a 'lexical' presupposition:
Mike: What's up?
Annie: I've stopped smoking – although I've never smoked.

(c) Cancelling a generalized implicature:
Mike: What's happened to the shampoo?
Annie: I used most of it – actually, I used all of it.

(d) Cancelling a particularized implicature:
Mike: Are you coming to the party?
Annie: My parents are in town – but I am coming.

Comment

When a speaker cancels a presupposition, the results usually sound rather contradictory or incoherent. However, when both generalized and particularized implicatures are cancelled, the results usually sound much more 'normal'.

There is a further level to the analysis of speaker meaning which we have not explored yet. For example, dialogue (c) could also be analysed as Mike's **accusation** followed by Annie's **confession.** In the next two units we will be looking at this level of analysis.

SUMMARY

- We have distinguished two types of conversational implicatures: generalized and particularized.
- Generalized implicatures can be drawn with very little 'inside' knowledge. If you heard a tape recording of the conversation but knew nothing about the participants or the physical characteristics of the context, you could still draw those implicatures. They are closely connected to the degree of informativeness that we normally expect a speaker's utterance to provide.
- Scalar implicatures are a special type of generalized implicature where the inference is made by reference to a scale of values, one of which has been chosen by the speaker. The speaker's choice implicates 'not the higher values'.

- Particularized implicatures require not only general knowledge but also knowledge which is particular or 'local' to the speaker and the hearer, and often to the physical context of the utterance as well.
- Both generalized and particularized implicatures differ from presuppositions in that they sound much less contradictory when they are cancelled by the speaker.

FURTHER EXERCISES ✎

5.6 Apply the cancellation test we used in **Exercise 5.5** to decide whether each of the inferences in brackets is a presupposition or an implicature.

(a) Linda: What's with Jean?
     Jen: She discovered that her central heating's broken. ('Her central heating is broken')

(b) Terry: How do you like your bath?
     Phil: Warm. ('I don't like it hot')

(c) Annie: What do you think of this necklace and bracelet?
     Mike: The bracelet is beautiful. ('The necklace is not beautiful')

(d) Lois: Has the kitchen been painted?
     Gabriela: Tom's away. ('No')

(e) Jane: Have you seen my sweater?
     Steve: There's a sweater on the sofa. ('It's not Steve's sweater')

(f) Mike: How come Mary's all dressed up?
     Annie: We're going to the D-E-N-T-I-S-T. ('Mary hates the dentist')

(g) Austin: It works now.
     Barbara: When did Eric fix it? ('Eric fixed it')

5.7 Which of the inferences in **Exercise 5.6** are generalized implicatures? Which ones are particularized implicatures?

SUPPLE-MENTARY EXERCISES ✎

5.8 Apply the cancellation test we used in **Exercises 5.5** and **5.6** to decide whether each of the inferences in brackets is a presupposition or an implicature. For the implicatures, decide whether they are generalized or particularized.

(a) Mike: I heard about the mess.
     Dave: Yeah, Steve really regrets sending that e-mail. ('Steve sent that e-mail')

(b) Patrick: I didn't take it.
    Virginia: Why do you always lie? ('You always lie')

(c) Doris: Did Carmen like the party?
    Dave: She left after an hour. ('She didn't like the party')

(d) Mat: How did you do on those exams?
    Chris: I failed physics. ('I didn't fail the others')

(e) Reporter: Senator, what is the present state of your marriage?
    Senator: Well, we, I think have been able to make some very good progress and it's – I would say that it's – it's – it's delightful that we're able to – to share the time and the relationship that we – that we do share. ('The marriage is not in a good state')

(f) Steve: Did you buy the car?
    Ed: It cost twice as much as I thought it would. ('Ed didn't buy the car')

(g) Maggie: The bathroom's flooded!
    James: Someone must have left the tap on. ('It wasn't James who left the tap on')

5.9   For the particularized implicatures in **Exercises 5.6** and **5.8**, what sort of particular or 'local' knowledge is needed to draw that implicature? What sorts of general knowledge do they require? Try writing scenarios where changing the 'local' knowledge would lead to quite different implicatures.

5.10   We have pointed out that generalized implicatures tend to be based on a flouting of the quantity maxim. That is, on the surface they are noticeably less informative than we would expect. What maxim or maxims were flouted in each of the particularized implicatures in **Exercise 5.6**?

⊂ **DISCUSSION QUESTIONS**

5.11   There is a semantic relationship between words called hyponymy. Here are some examples of hyponymy:

Hyponym	Super-ordinate
rose	flower
salmon	fish
hammer	tool

In the relation of HYPONYMY the meaning of the SUPER-ORDINATE term is included in the meaning of the HYPONYM. That is, the

Hyponomy
Super-ordinate
Hyponym

meaning of *rose* includes the meaning of *flower*. We can also say that the hyponym is 'a kind of' the super-ordinate. For example, a rose is a kind of flower. Note also that the entailment relationship between hyponyms and their super-ordinates is one-way (see **Exercise 2.4**). For example, *I picked a rose* entails *I picked a flower*, but *I picked a flower* does not necessarily entail *I picked a rose*. Discuss the types of implicatures that can be drawn in the following dialogues which exploit the relation of hyponymy. Would you class some of these as generalized implicatures?

(a) Mike: Did you buy her a rose?
    Annie: I bought her a flower.

(b) Jane: There's salmon on the menu.
    Steve: I don't like fish.

(c) Ed: Be careful of that sofa.
    Meridyth: It's a piece of furniture, Dad.

(d) Mat: So you've taken up teaching.
    Chris: It's a job.

Co-ordinating conjunctions

5.12   In **Discussion Question 3.11** we looked at some conventional meanings for *and*. Look back at the examples given there. Could we characterize *and* as creating different implicatures in each case? Explore the effects of two other CO-ORDINATING CONJUNCTIONS, *but* and *or*. Here are some examples to get you started.

(a) Tom stayed but Mark left.
(b) Tom stayed but Bill stayed too.
(c) Stop that or I'll leave.
(d) Do you want milk or juice?

Auxiliary verbs

5.13   Can AUXILIARY VERBS like *should, may, might, must, will* create scalar implicatures? For example, compare You should wash the dishes and You must wash the dishes.

FURTHER READING

The idea that presuppositions do not 'survive' cancellation as well as implicatures can be problematic. For more on this debate see:

Simpson, 1993, pp. 133–40.

Grice's work was an important first step in systematically examining how hearers work to derive the ultimate message from the words that are actually uttered. He recognized that, of all the maxims, relevance was probably the most important, although he never really tackled the issue of how speakers and hearers actually assign relevance to particular pieces of information. Sperber and Wilson have carried this work forward by looking even more systematically at the various kinds of inferencing that take place in normal conversation. They suggest that all four maxims can be subsumed under relevance. See:

Sperber and Wilson, 1986 (quite challenging).

For a 'beginner's' introduction to Sperber and Wilson's theories:

Blakemore, 1992.

6

SPEECH ACTS

We look at inferences about what speakers are trying to accomplish with their utterances and introduce speech-act theory.

> The phenomenon to be discussed is very widespread and obvious, and it cannot fail to have been already noticed, at least here and there by others. Yet I have not found attention paid to it specifically.
>
> (Austin, 1975, p. 1)

Thus began a series of lectures by the philosopher, J.L. Austin, which were given at Harvard University in 1955 and later published under the title *How to Do Things with Words*.

EXERCISE ✎

6.1 Decide if you could perform each of the following actions by either speaking or physical gesture:

(a) Congratulate someone.
(b) Call someone's attention to the television set.
(c) Forbid someone to enter a room.

Comment

(a) Yes. By saying Congratulations! or by giving someone a pat on the back or the thumbs up sign. (b) Yes. By saying Look at the television or by pointing to it. (c) Yes. By saying I forbid you to enter or by wagging your finger at the person (as often happens to inappropriately dressed visitors to Italian churches).

The proverbs *Actions speak louder than words* and *Easier said than done* seem to make a clear distinction between speaking and acting. However, Austin pointed out that, contrary to popular belief, there is often no clear distinction between the two. He was one of the first modern scholars to recognize that 'words' are in themselves actions and that these SPEECH ACTS can and should be systematically studied.

Speech acts

✐ EXERCISE

6.2 One way of describing what the following utterances do is to say that they describe a state of affairs. But think of some contexts where each of these assertions does much more than simply describe a state of affairs:

(a) There's a spider in your hair.
(b) Someone's eaten all the ice-cream.
(c) I've got a gun.
(d) You're an idiot.
(e) I need the salt.

Comment

(a) Your friend is about to run his fingers through his hair: **warning**. (b) You confront your flat mate about the missing ice-cream: **accusing**. (c) Spoken by someone in a mask to a bank cashier: **threatening**. (d) You have been offended and want revenge: **insulting**. (e) You say this to someone at the table who is sitting near the salt: **requesting**. When contextualized, these utterances are doing far more than simply asserting. This is not to say that assertion is not involved in these utterances, but rather that there is a more basic purpose behind them. Austin wanted to counter a commonly held view by semanticists that the sole purpose of making assertions is to describe some state of affairs. That view is sometimes called the DESCRIPTIVE FALLACY.

Descriptive fallacy

So far we have restricted ourselves to analysing utterances consisting of declarative sentences, but utterances based on imperative and interrogative sentences can also be analysed in terms of what the utterance **does.**

✐ EXERCISE

6.3 Classify each of the following utterances as interrogative, imperative or declarative (see **Exercise 3.1** for examples of each type). Then decide what the speaker is using the utterance to do.

(a) You can pass the milk.
(b) Why don't you pass the milk?
(c) Have you got the milk?
(d) I could use the milk.

(e) Get me the milk.
(f) Send the milk down here.

Comment

Despite the fact that (e) and (f) are imperatives, (b) and (c) are interrogatives and (a) and (d) are declaratives, all six utterances can be acts of **requesting** (milk in this case).

Locution
Illocution

Illocutionary force

Austin pointed out that in analysing a speech act, we need to make a distinction between the LOCUTION and the ILLOCUTION. The locution is the actual form of words used by the speaker and their semantic meaning. The illocution (or ILLOCUTIONARY FORCE) is what the speaker is doing by uttering those words: **commanding**, **offering**, **promising**, **threatening**, **thanking,** etc. Below is an example of how this two-way analysis can work for Mike's utterance to Annie: Give me some cash.

> LOCUTION: Mike uttered the words *Give me some cash* which can be semantically paraphrased as: 'Hand some money over to me', with *me* referring to *Mike*.
> ILLOCUTION: Mike performed the **act of requesting** Annie to give him some cash.

We need to distinguish between the illocution and the locution because, as we saw in **Exercise 6.3**, different locutions can have the same illocutionary force. Similarly, the same locution can have different illocutionary forces depending on the context. For example, It's cold in here could either be a **request** to close the window or an **offer** to close the window.

Perlocution

Austin also distinguished a third part of a speech act, the PERLOCU-TION. This is the actual result of the locution. It may or may not be what the speaker wants to happen but it is nevertheless caused by the locution. For example, Mike's utterance could have any of the following perlocutions: 'Mike persuaded Annie to give him the money'; 'Annie refused to give him the money'; 'Annie was offended', etc. As you can see, the perlocution is defined by the hearer's reaction.

EXERCISE ✎

6.4 Look at the following pairs of utterances. What difference do you notice between the utterances in each pair?

1(a) I promise to be there.
1(b) I'll be there.

2(a) I admit I was foolish.
2(b) I was foolish.

3(a) I warn you, this gun is loaded.
3(b) This gun is loaded.

4(a) I apologize.
4(b) I'm sorry.

Austin made an interesting observation. Some utterances not only perform a speech act over and above simple assertion, they also simultaneously describe the speech act itself. He called these PERFORMATIVE utterances (the (a) utterances in each pair). They contrast with other utterances which may be performing the same act but do not contain a PERFORMATIVE VERB that explicitly describes the intended speech act. Rather, the hearer is left to infer the speaker's intention. Austin called these CONSTATIVE utterances (the (b) utterances in each pair). Below we illustrate the two types. The underlined words are the PERFORMATIVE VERBS.

Comment

Performative

Performative verb

Constative

Performative verbs

Performative	*Constative*
I <u>promise</u> I'll be there.	I'll be there.
I <u>admit</u> I was foolish.	I was foolish.
I <u>warn</u> you, this gun is loaded.	This gun is loaded.
I <u>apologize</u>.	I'm sorry.
I <u>thank</u> you.	I'm very grateful.
I <u>order</u> you to sit down.	You must sit down.

However, the fact that an utterance contains a performative verb does not necessarily make the utterance itself performative, as we will see in the next exercise.

✏ EXERCISE

6.5 In each of the groups below only the (a) utterances would be performative in Austin's view. Think about why the (b) and (c) utterances would not be classed as performative.

1(a) I admit I was wrong.
1(b) I think I was wrong.
1(c) I know I was wrong.

2(a) I apologize to you.
2(b) I amuse you.
2(c) I flatter you.

3(a) We promise to leave.
3(b) He admits he was silly.
3(c) I warned you to stop.

In group **1** the problem with (b) and (c) is that while admitting is an action that can be performed by speaking, thinking and knowing are not. So, *think* and *know* are not performative verbs.

Comment

In group **2** *apologize*, *amuse* and *flatter* all describe things we can do with speech. However, to be performative, the verb must describe an action which is under the control of the speaker. We can potentially amuse or flatter someone with speech but the ultimate decision to be amused or flattered rests with the hearer. Compare: (a) I'm trying to apologize. (b) I'm trying to amuse you. (c) I'm trying to flatter you. Only in (a) is there a clear implication that the speaker is being prevented from speaking (or being heard). One way of thinking about this is that *apologize* refers to an illocution while *flatter* and *amuse* refer to perlocutions.

In group **3** each of the verbs is performative. However in (b) the subject of the verb is not the speaker: *I* or *we*. He admits he was silly simply states what 'he' is doing but does not **perform** his act of admission. Even when the subject of the performative verb is *I* or *we*, as in (c) the verb must be in the simple present tense not the past tense. For example, if you were expecting an apology from me would you prefer I apologize or I apologized?

EXERCISE ✎

6.6 Insert the word *hereby* before the verb in all nine utterances in **Exercise 6.5**. For example: I hereby I admit I was wrong; I hereby think I was wrong. Does this produce odd results in some cases? Why?

Comment

Although *hereby* does not frequently occur in ordinary conversation and can make any utterance seem a bit stilted, it seems to sound particularly odd when the utterance is not performative. The 'hereby test' is quite a reliable one.

Austin's distinction between performative and constative utterances is not without problems, as another philosopher of language, J.R. Searle, has pointed out. How do we interpret I'll be there on its own as a promise? Austin had proposed that this can be expanded to a full form including the perfomative verb – I promise I'll be there. In Searle's view, this made the distinction between performatives and constatives rather artificial, since in theory any constative utterance can be expanded to a performative one. Besides, this does not really tackle the question of how the hearer would assign the appropriate illocutionary force to utterances which do not contain performative verbs. How do we know that the speaker means 'I **promise** I'll be back' rather than 'I **threaten** I'll be back'? What about Coffee? How does the hearer 'compute' from this one word 'I **offer** you a coffee'? How do we manage to interpret Can you pass the milk? not as 'I **inquire** if you are able to pass the milk' but rather as 'I **request** you to pass the milk'. We will be exploring these issues in the next unit.

SUMMARY

- Utterances can be analysed as speech acts, a framework originally proposed by J.L. Austin.
- Speech acts can be analysed on three levels: the **locution** (the words the speaker uses); the **illocution**, or **illocutionary force** (what the speaker is doing by using those words); the **perlocution** (the effect of those words on the hearer).
- Austin proposed that utterances can be classified as **performative** or **constative**. Performatives like I apologize simultaneously state and perform the illocution. Constatives can also be used to perform an illocution but, unlike performatives, they do not explicitly name the intended illocutionary act.

FURTHER EXERCISES

6.7 Decide whether each of the utterances below is performative, and if not, why not.

 (a) You congratulate me.
 (b) I envy you.
 (c) I command you to put out that cigarette.
 (d) I warned you not to go.
 (e) Put your toys away!
 (f) We convince everyone with our arguments.

6.8 Using the locution, illocution, perlocution analysis in the discussion following **Exercise 6.3**, analyse Steve's utterance.

 Jane: You've interrupted me again!
 Steve: I was rude.

SUPPLE- MENTARY EXERCISES

6.9 Give as many different illocutions as you can for the locutions: I'm sorry and This gun is loaded. Describe the context in which each of those illocutions would apply.

6.10 Choose a particular illocutionary force (e.g. **apology**, **threat**, **request**) and give at least five different locutions which could express that force.

6.11 Give three possible perlocutions for the locution: I love coffee.

6.12 The expressions below refer to 'things we can do with words'. Which ones focus on the speaker's action and which ones focus on the hearer's reaction?

(a) offend
(b) mock
(c) offer condolences
(d) convince
(e) argue
(f) console

6.13 Find at least one performative verb that could produce the perlocution referred to by each of the following verbs:

(a) scare
(b) persuade
(c) confuse
(d) entertain
(e) impress
(f) placate
(g) inspire

DISCUSSION QUESTIONS

6.14 Performative utterances can be worded in such a way that they do not require *I* or *we* as the subject. Apply the 'hereby test' to each of the following to determine which ones are performative. What allows them to pass the test?

(a) I forbid you to spit on the pavement.
(b) Spitting on the pavement is forbidden.
(c) Spitting on the pavement was forbidden.
(d) You are forbidden to spit on the pavement.
(e) Spitting on the pavement is inconsiderate.
(f) You must not spit on the pavement.

6.15 Miscommunication can result when the hearer has miscalculated the intended illocution. This often forms the basis of humour as in the following rather awful joke where a **complaint** is (deliberately?) misinterpreted as **praise**.

Customer: Waiter! There's a fly in my soup.
Waiter: Don't worry, there's no extra charge.

Find examples of jokes with a similar basis.

6.16 Look in a thesaurus for the verbs related to the speech acts of *confession* and *apology*. How many did you find? Were some more negatively 'loaded' than others?

6.17 Following on from **Exercise 6.1**, think of at least five acts that you could perform by using either words or gestures. In the case of performing the act by gesture, is this ever dependent on speech being used at some point in the event? Think about bidding at an auction, for example. Can you think of any acts that can only be performed by using words?

6.18 In **Exercise 6.6** you might have felt that the addition of *hereby* to He admits he was silly sounded slightly less odd than it did with the other non-performative utterances. Can you think of a special situation where He hereby admits he was silly could be considered performative?

For an annotated version of Austin's original lectures:

> Austin, 1975.

For introductions to speech-act theory:

> Stubbs, 1983, Chapter 8.
> Coulthard, 1985, Chapter 2.

Austin's proposal that speaking can be analysed as action has made a major contribution to pragmatics. His basic analytic framework has stimulated an enormous amount of thinking and research about a previously neglected but very important area of interpersonal meaning. However, some of his ideas, particularly his distinction between performative and constative utterances, have attracted a considerable amount of criticism. See:

> Blakemore, 1992, Chapter 6.
> Leech, 1983, Chapters 8 and 9.

FURTHER READING

7 MORE ABOUT SPEECH ACTS

> We introduce felicity conditions and look at ways of classifying and identifying speech acts.

If you do that, I won't eat my dessert.
(Matteo Peccei, age 3)

As soon as our son (a champion dessert eater) uttered those words, he looked quite puzzled. He realized that his attempt to 'threaten' his parents had somehow gone horribly wrong, but why? Austin would have said that Matteo's threat was not 'felicitous' because, among other things, a threat should involve an action that is undesirable to the hearer rather than to the speaker. Austin's idea that it is possible to state the necessary conditions for a particular illocution to 'count' was developed further by John Searle (1971). In the next exercise, we

Felicity conditions will look at some of the types of FELICITY CONDITIONS for a promise.

EXERCISE

7.1 What might make each of these 'promises' infelicitous?

(a) Ti prometto di pulire la cucina. ['I promise you that I'll clean up the kitchen' spoken to someone who the speaker knows does not understand Italian.]

(b) I promise that I'll punch you in the nose.

(c) I promise that the sun will come up tomorrow.

(d) I promise that I started the dishwasher.

(e) I promise that you'll make a wonderful dessert.

(f) I promise that I'll jump over that skyscraper if I pass my exam.

The problem with (a) is that the hearer cannot understand what the speaker has actually said. The speaker must not be acting nonsensically or pretending to be someone else and the hearer must be capable of understanding the locution. Searle called these GENERAL CONDITIONS because they apply to all types of illocutions. The problems with (b) and (c) involve what Searle called the PREPARATORY CONDITIONS. In the case of a promise it has to be about something that would not ordinarily happen. And it must be about an act that would be beneficial to the hearer.

The problems with (d) and (e) have to do with the 'content' of the promise. A promise has to be a about a future act. In (d) *started* is in the past tense. And, it must be about an act performed by the **speaker**. In (e) *make a wonderful dessert* is an act that will be performed by the hearer. These are called the CONTENT CONDITIONS. Different illocutions will have different content conditions. Related to the preparatory conditions is the SINCERITY CONDITION. That is, the speaker must be sincere. In the case of a promise, the speaker must genuinely intend to carry out the act mentioned. This is clearly not the case in (f) unless the speaker is Superman.

Of course, not every utterance includes a performative verb like *promise*. Yet we normally manage to infer what the speaker intends. To start tackling this problem, Searle proposed that speech acts could be grouped into general categories based not on performative verbs but on the relationship between 'the words' and 'the world' and on who is responsible for making that relationship work. Within each category there can be a variety of different illocutions, but the members of each group share a similar relationship of 'fit' between the words and the world. We'll start with three very basic categories and some of the different illocutions that would fall into that category:

> REPRESENTATIVES – Speakers represent external reality by making their words fit the world as they believe it to be (*stating, describing, affirming*).
>
> COMMISSIVES – Speakers commit themselves to a future act which will make the world fit their words (*promising, vowing, threatening, offering*).
>
> DIRECTIVES – Speakers direct hearers to perform some future act which will make the world fit the speaker's words (*commanding, ordering, requesting, warning, suggesting*).

Comment

General conditions

Preparatory conditions

Content conditions

Sincerity condition

Representatives

Commissives

Directives

✐ **EXERCISE**

7.2   In each of the following dialogues, decide whether the second speaker's utterance is a representative, a commissive, or a directive.

(a) Jane: Coco's sick.
    Steve: I'll take her to the vet.
(b) Mike: What's the weather like in Dallas?
    Annie: It's raining.

(c)   Ed: The garage is a mess.

       Faye: Clean it up!

Comment

(a)–(c) were fairly easy to classify according to this system. Steve's act was a commissive. Annie's act was a representative. Fay's act was a directive.

EXERCISE ✎

7.3 Look at the second speakers' utterances in next the two dialogues. Can these be easily classified using the categories of representative, commissive or directive?

(d)   Carmen: You've thrown away the paper.

       Dave: I'm sorry.

(e)   Patrick: I got a new Nintendo game.

       Virginia: Who from?

Comment

Dave's utterance in (d) is a statement like It's raining but it represents the speaker's emotions rather than the 'outside world'. An utterance like this is typically used as an apology. Searle proposed a special category for speech acts that focus primarily on representing the speaker's feelings: EXPRESSIVES through which speakers express

Expressives

their feelings by making their words fit their internal psychological world. Expressives can refer to the hearer or to some other aspect of the world, but their focus is the speaker's feeling about it. For example You're very kind or This wine is awful would be classed as expressives (*thanking, apologizing, congratulating, condoling*).

In a way, Virginia's utterance in (e) is 'directing' Patrick to provide her with information about who gave him the Nintendo game. Searle had originally classed questions like this as directives. Apart from the idea that requesting information from hearers is rather different from requesting that they perform an action, some questions are much more directive than others. Compare Have they appointed a new director? to Can you hand me the pen? Leech (1983) proposed an extra category to deal with requests for information:

Rogatives

ROGATIVES through which speakers ask for information. In rogatives the hearer rather than the speaker will make the words fit the world (*asking, querying, questioning*).

EXERCISE ✎

7.4 How would you describe the relationship between the words and the world in the following utterances? Do any of the categories we have discussed so far capture this relationship?

(a) I now pronounce you husband and wife.
(b) I name this ship 'Buster Brown'.
(c) I sentence you to 10 years in prison.

In (a)–(c) the mere act of uttering the words has changed the world. **Comment**
A couple are now married. A ship is now named 'Buster Brown'.
Someone is now a prisoner for 10 years. These kinds of speech acts
are quite special in that they can only 'count' if the speaker has the
appropriate authority to perform these acts. Searle called these:
DECLARATIONS. The speaker utters words that in themselves change **Declarations**
the world (*naming ships*, *marriages*, *sentencing*, *a referee's 'calls'*).
   Table 1 shows the similarities and differences between the speech
act categories that we have been discussing.

Table 1 The relation between 'words' and 'the world'

Speech-act category	Relation between 'the words' and 'the world'	Who is responsible for the relation
Declarations	the words change the world	speaker
Representatives	the words fit the world ('outside' world)	speaker
Expressives	the words fit the world ('psychological' world)	speaker
Rogatives	the words fit the world	hearer
Commissives	the world will fit the words	speaker
Directives	the world will fit the words	hearer

✎ **EXERCISE**

7.5 Look at each of these pairs of utterances. Classify the likely
speech-act type expressed by the (a) utterance using the categories
in **Table 1**. Satisfy yourself that, given the right context, the (b) utterance in each pair could also be used to carry out that type of speech
act. Why does the first utterance in each pair seem a more 'direct'
way of performing the act?

1(a) Go away.
1(b) My essay is due tomorrow morning.

2(a) Put your jacket on.
2(b) Did you put your jacket on?

3(a) Be quiet.
3(b) I'm very upset that so many of you are talking.

4(a) The Democrats won.
4(b) Have you heard that the Democrats won?

5(a) Have you been fired?
5(b) Someone said you got fired.

6(a) I'll pay you back.
6(b) Authors always pay their debts.

Comment

1(a), 2(a) and 3(a) are directives. 4(a) is a representative, 5(a) is a rogative, and 6(a) is a commissive. Note that the speakers did not have to say I order you to go away, I state that the Democrats won, or I ask whether you have been fired. The direct interpretation came from other linguistic features of the utterance which we recognize as typical for that type of speech act. Table 2 summarizes these features.

Table 2 Typical linguistic expressions of speech acts

Speech-act category	Typical expression	Example
Declarations	declarative structure with speaker as subject and a performative verb in simple present tense	We find the defendant guilty. I resign.
Representatives	declarative structure	Tom's eating grapes. Bill was an accountant.
Expressives	declarative structure with words referring to feelings	I'm sorry to hear that. This beer is disgusting.
Directives	imperative sentence	Sit down! Fasten your seat belts.
Rogatives	interrogative structure	Where did he go? Is she leaving?
Commissives	declarative structure with speaker subject and future time expressed	I'll call you tonight. We're going to turn you in.

EXERCISE

7.6 This time look at the (b) utterance in each of the pairs in **Exercise 7.5**. Using **Table 2**, decide what type of speech act they 'look like'.

Comment

1(b) looks like a representative. In fact, Searle would say that it **is** a representative, but in this context it can also 'do the work' of a directive. In 2(b) we have a rogative functioning as a directive; in 3(b) an expressive functioning as a directive; in 4(b) a rogative functioning as a representative; in 5(b) a representative functioning as a rogative; and in 6(b) a representative functioning as a commissive.

This led Searle to a further distinction between speech acts. In DIRECT SPEECH ACTS there is a direct relationship between their linguistic structure and the work they are doing. In INDIRECT SPEECH ACTS the speech act is performed indirectly through the performance of another speech act. So, how do hearers know what the 'real' illocutionary force is when presented with an indirect speech act? This is where felicity conditions can be quite useful.

Direct speech acts
Indirect speech acts

Searle observed that in an indirect speech act, even though the surface form looks like a particular direct speech act, one (or more) of the felicity conditions for that act have been **obviously violated**. At the same time, one (or more) of the felicity conditions for the 'real', underlying, and therefore indirect speech act have been questioned or mentioned by the locution, giving a hint as to the true illocutionary force. If the remaining felicity conditions for the 'real' speech act are fulfilled, then the speaker will interpret the locution as such.

✐ **EXERCISE**

7.7 Try your hand at writing some felicity conditions for a 'true' or 'felicitous' directive.

Your answers probably looked something like this:

Comment

- The speaker must be in a position to direct the hearer to perform the act.
- The directed act must not be something which has already happened or would happen anyway.
- The directed act must be something the hearer is willing or obligated to carry out if asked.
- The directed act must be something which the hearer is capable of carrying out.
- The directed act must be something which is needed by or desirable to the speaker.

✐ **EXERCISE**

7.8 Now write two key felicity conditions for a 'felicitous' rogative.

For a rogative:

Comment

- The speaker must not already have the information requested.
- The speaker must have reason to believe that the hearer can supply the information.

EXERCISE

7.9   A mother is standing by the door as her child starts to go out without his jacket and says: Did you put your jacket on? Using the felicity conditions for directives and rogatives, explain why the mother's utterance would be interpreted as an indirect directive.

Comment

Did you put your jacket on? looks superficially like a rogative given its interrogative form, but it violates the key felicity condition that the speaker does not already know the answer to the question (the mother can see that the child does not have his jacket on). On the other hand, the utterance explicitly queries one of the felicity conditions for a directive: the directed act must be something that has not already happened or would happen anyway. Assuming that the remaining felicity conditions for a valid directive are met (look at the remaining felicity conditions for a directive and satisfy yourself that this is the case), the hearer will interpret this as an indirect directive to put on the jacket.

If the child simply replied No I didn't without putting on the jacket, it would normally be interpreted as a deliberate refusal to carry out a directive. Often when hearers receive this kind of indirect directive they respond to the rogative by answering No while simultaneously carrying out the indirect directive.

You may have already observed that, particularly in the case of directives, there is a strong link between politeness and the degree of directness. We will be exploring this issue in the next unit.

SUMMARY

- Speech acts can be grouped into general categories which are based on the relationship between 'the words' and 'the world' and on who is responsible for bringing about the relationship.
- Speech acts can also be classified as direct or indirect. In a **direct speech act** there is a direct relationship between its linguistic structure and the work it is doing. In **indirect speech acts** the speech act is performed indirectly through the performance of another speech act.
- **Felicity conditions** are sets of necessary conditions for an illocution to 'count'.
- The true illocutionary force of an indirect speech act can be inferred from the fact that one or more of the felicity conditions of the 'surface' speech act have been obviously violated, while at the same time one or more of the felicity conditions for the indirect speech act have been mentioned or questioned.

✎ FURTHER
EXERCISES

7.10   In **Exercises 7.2** and **7.3** you were asked to identify the speech acts of the second speakers using the categories in **Table 1**. Now go back and do the same thing for the first speakers' utterances.

7.11   An utterance that looks superficially like a directive because of its imperative form, but is indirectly realizing another type of speech act, is sometimes called a PSEUDO-DIRECTIVE. Label each of the following utterances as direct directive, indirect directive or pseudo-directive. For a pseudo-directive state the true illocutionary force. Give your reasons in each case, making use of the felicity-condition framework.

Pseudo-directive

(a) Mother to child: Please pick up your clothes.
(b) Mother to child: You haven't made your bed!
(c) Speaker has just been thanked: Don't mention it.

✎ SUPPLE-
MENTARY
EXERCISES

7.12   Using the answer to **Exercise 7.9**, show how Can you be quiet? would be interpreted as an indirect directive.

7.13   Apply the direct directive/indirect directive/pseudo-directive analysis used in **Exercise 7.11** to the following:

(a) Burglary victim to police officer in a ransacked house: Officer, look at the mess they've made!
(b) Mourner to bereaved: Please accept my deepest sympathy.
(c) Mother to child: How many times have I asked you to clean your room?
(d) Mother to child: You should clean up your room.
(e) Waiter to diner: Enjoy your meal.
(f) Sacked worker to boss: Drop dead!

7.14   Look again at the utterances in **Exercise 7.1**. Since we concluded that they were not promises, what were they?

7.15   Take the example utterances in **Table 2** and construct a context where each of these could be used to perform indirectly some other type of speech act.

DISCUSSION
QUESTIONS

7.16   It is possible to write felicity conditions that apply to all the members of a category. For example, all commissives share certain felicity conditions such as they must refer in some way to a future act which will be performed by the speaker. However, different illo-cutions in that category will have special felicity conditions that distinguish them from each other. For example, a threat involves an action undesirable to the hearer, while a promise involves a desir-able one. Coulthard (1985) has proposed that it is very difficult to write felicity conditions for expressives in general because they are usually used to perform some other act over and above simply repre-senting the speaker's psychological state. Do you agree?

7.17 Try writing a set of felicity conditions for each of the following illocutionary acts.

- (a) thanking
- (b) commanding
- (c) naming a ship
- (d) apologizing
- (e) congratulating
- (f) performing a marriage

You will probably find that, for some of these, the sincerity condi-tion was a bit problematic. For example, does an apology have to be sincere in order to count as an apology? In Parliament an MP says I apologize for calling my honourable friend a liar to avoid being ejected from the House. The mere form of words is enough, even when everyone present knows that the MP is not remotely sorry. Content conditions can also be a problem in some of these. For example, can You're hitched! be substituted for I now pronounce you man and wife?

7.18 Leech (1983) proposed that declarations are not really communicative acts at all, but simply the linguistic part of a larger **ritual** and as such do not really belong in **Table 1**. Do you agree?

7.19 Do we need to give consideration to paralinguistic elements? Can an act of *thanking* be felicitous if spoken with clenched teeth, narrowed eyes, and a rather vicious tone of voice?

7.20 Searle acknowledged that there are several 'grey areas' in his classification system. Using the classifications in **Table 1**, where would you put *boasting, complaining, accusing, deploring*? What distinguishes *confiding* from *announcing*, both of which would belong to the general class of representatives? Is *advising* a representative or a directive?

For Searle in the 'original' (quite challenging):

>Searle, 1971, 1979.

For a beginner level discussion of Searle's thinking with a short extract from his work:

>Yule, 1996.

For alternative ways of classifying speech acts and identifying indirect speech acts:

>Labov and Fanshel, 1977.

For how Grice's work on conversational implicature relates to speech-act theory:

>Levinson, 1983.

8   POLITENESS

> We look at the importance of politeness in determining how we structure and interpret utterances.

> Rude I am in speech and little blessed with the soft phrase of peace.
>
> > (Shakespeare, *Othello*, Act 1, Scene 2)

> A child who is not allowed to say anything but 'No, thank you' at home, will not mortify his mother in public by screaming 'I hate steak, I want ice-cream!'
>
> > (Emily Post, *Etiquette*, 1922)

> Instancing the rudeness of waiters, Andrew Billen quoted one as saying 'I don't know, can you?' in reply to his question, 'Can we order now?'. If Mr. Billen had been taught good manners as a child, he would have asked 'May we order now?' ... Mr. Billen should learn proper manners himself before complaining about the lack of niceness in others.
>
> > (Letter to the editor of the *Evening Standard*, 25 November 1998)

We clearly attach great importance to 'speaking politely'. This aspect of the communicative process was largely ignored by Austin, Searle and Grice. Yet, the need to be polite can often account for why we choose to imply rather than assert an idea or why we choose to use an indirect directive like Well, I really must get on with my work now, rather than a direct directive like Go home.

 **EXERCISE**

8.1 Below are five utterances with an imperative structure. Assume that each one would be spoken by the host to a guest. Rearrange them in order of politeness, starting with the least polite. Think about what made some of these utterances seem more polite than others.

- (a) Take a look at this.
- (b) Clean up the kitchen floor.
- (c) Pass the salt.
- (d) Have some more cake.
- (e) Peel these potatoes.

Comment

Most people rank the utterances like this:

- (b) Clean up the kitchen floor.
- (e) Peel these potatoes.
- (c) Pass the salt.
- (a) Take a look at this.
- (d) Have some more cake.

In each of these cases, the speaker is requesting some sort of action from the hearer. What you probably noticed is that the smaller the 'cost' of the action for the hearer, the more polite the speaker sounds. In fact, by the time we get to Have some more cake, there is a positive benefit to the hearer and we interpret this as an offer rather than a request. Leech (1983) proposed a TACT MAXIM which reflects this tendency. It can be summarized as: **Minimize the cost to other; maximize the benefit to other.**

Tact maxim

✎ **EXERCISE**

8.2 Here are three possible requests for the same action. Again, assume that each one would be spoken by the host to a guest and rearrange them in order of politeness, starting with the least polite. Think about what made some of these utterances seem more polite than others.

- (a) Could I possibly ask you to set the table?
- (b) Set the table.
- (c) Can you set the table?

Comment

Most people rank the utterances like this:

- (b) Set the table.
- (c) Can you set the table?
- (a) Could I possibly ask you to set the table?

What you probably noticed is that as these requests become more polite, they also become more indirect. Utterance (b) uses an imperative structure making it a direct directive. Utterance (c) uses an interrogative structure, phrasing a directive as a rogative, (a question about the hearer's ability to carry out the action). Utterance (a) is even more indirect since the speaker is technically asking permission to make a request. What is happening here is that, as the request becomes more indirect, the speaker is making it less and less obvious that she expects the hearer to comply. On the surface, at least, this provides greater freedom for the hearer to refuse the request. Leech also observed that the higher the cost of the directed act, the more likely it is for the speaker to use an indirect form. Most people judge **Can you pass the salt?** as more polite than **Can you clean up the kitchen floor?** So far we have been discussing directives and commissives. But the relationship between politeness and indirectness can also apply to representatives.

EXERCISE

8.3 In each of the following dialogues, there are three alternative responses for the second speaker. Put them in increasing order of politeness.

1   Meridyth: Well, I've done it. I've dyed my hair blonde.
    Ed: (a) You look beautiful.
          (b) You look awful.
          (c) You look amazing.

2   Tom: Do you like the wine I picked out?
    Gabriela: (a) It's Italian, isn't it?
               (b) Yes, I do.
               (c) Not really.

3   Jean: What did the students say about my teaching?
    Linda: (a) Let's hope none of them are lawyers.
             (b) Some students were very positive.
             (c) Pretty bad.

Comment

Most people rank the responses like this:

1(b) You look awful.
1(c) You look amazing.
1(a) You look beautiful.
2(c) Not really.
2(a) It's Italian, isn't it?
2(b) Yes, I do.
3(c) Pretty bad.
3(a) Let's hope none of them are lawyers.
3(b) Some students were very positive.

Two things emerge here. First of all, and not surprisingly, saying something good about the other person is much more polite than saying something bad. Leech called this the APPROBATION MAXIM which can be summarized as: **Minimize dispraise of other; maximize praise of other.** Second, if you have to say something bad about (dispraise) the other, it seems to be more polite to take an indirect route. Leech pointed out that, while speakers need to observe the maxim of quality (be truthful) in representatives, they often find that this conflicts not so much with one of Grice's other three maxims, but rather with the need to be polite. To resolve this clash, speakers imply a criticism rather than baldly state it.

Approbation maxim

In **dialogue 1**, You look amazing probably implies that Ed did not like the blonde hair. He does this by flouting the maxim of quantity (be maximally informative). The ambiguity of *amazing* (amazing for its beauty or amazing for its awfulness?) allows the speaker to be truthful and yet somewhat more polite than the direct answer You look awful. In **dialogue 2**, It's Italian, isn't it? implies a less than whole-hearted endorsement of the wine by failing to be maximally informative, 'answering' a question with another question, and by failing to be maximally relevant since the topic was the wine's taste not its country of origin. Still, Gabriela was being more polite than coming right out with the fact that she did not like it. In **dialogue 3**, both (a) Let's hope none of them are lawyers and (b) Some students were very positive both imply rather than directly state that overall the student evaluations were not good and therefore are more polite than Pretty bad. What might make (b) more polite than (a) is that it allows Linda to maximize praise for Jean while still being truthful. However, not everyone rates (a) as less polite. A joking reply and the use of *let's* (*you* and *me*) can indicate a sense of solidarity between the speaker and the hearer. Too much attention to tact and approval can often seem like condescension. You might want to think about this aspect of politeness as you do the next exercise.

✏ **EXERCISE**

8.4 (a) If you and a close friend were having lunch, would you prefer to say Pass the salt or Would you mind passing me the salt? Which one would you use to a stranger at another table in a restaurant?

(b) If you wanted to ask your bank manager for a loan, would you prefer I'd like to ask for a loan of £500, or Lend me £500?

(c) Someone you have just met has come over for dinner and offers to help in the kitchen. Would you be more likely to say Here, peel these potatoes or You could peel these potatoes.

(d) If you had to evacuate a burning building would you say, Fire! Get out! or Fire! Might I possibly ask you to leave the building?

(e) Is an army sergeant being rude when he says **Sit down, Private**? Suppose you have arrived for a job interview and the interviewer stands up when you enter. Would you consider it rude to say to her **Sit down**? Would it be okay to say this to good friends when they drop by?

Comment

Leech observed that the relationship between indirectness and politeness can be quite complicated. The social distance between the speaker and the hearer, and the need to feel accepted by other people, can also have a significant effect on how we interpret the politeness of an utterance, and indeed how we structure our own utterances. We see in (a) that between friends an indirect and more formal directive like **Would you mind passing me the salt?** or **Could you please pass me the salt?** can sound rather unfriendly. However, with someone you do not know very well, this seems more appropriate. In (b) and (e) where there was a considerable power or status difference between speaker and hearer (another kind of social distance), we see a considerable difference in the acceptability of 'bald' directives. In the case of the military, the authority of a higher rank is so absolute that politeness does not really seem an appropriate criterion to apply. In (d) we notice that an urgent need for clarity can make very 'bald' directives, even to people we do not know very well, not only acceptable but highly desirable.

A framework to deal with these kinds of issues was developed by Brown and Levinson (1987). In their analysis, politeness involves us showing an awareness of other people's FACE WANTS. As used by these authors, FACE refers to our public self-image. There are two aspects to this self image.

Face wants
Face

Positive face

POSITIVE FACE refers to our need to be accepted and liked by others and our need to feel that our social group shares common goals. POSITIVE POLITENESS orients to preserving the positive face of other people. When we use positive politeness we use speech strategies that emphasize our solidarity with the hearer, such as informal pronunciation, shared dialect or slang expressions, nicknames, more frequent reference to speaker and hearer as *we*, and requests which are less indirect.

Positive politeness

Negative face

NEGATIVE FACE refers to our right to independence of action and our need not to be imposed on by others. (Note that *negative* does not mean *bad* here, simply an opposite term to *positive*.) NEGATIVE POLITENESS orients to preserving the negative face of other people. This is much more likely if there is a social distance between the speaker and hearer. When we use negative politeness, we use speech strategies that emphasize our deference for the hearer. Nicknames, slang and informal pronunciation tend to be avoided and requests tend to be more indirect and impersonal, often involving *could you ...* or *could I ask you to ...* or even referring to the hearer in the third person: *Students are asked not to put their essays in the staff*

Negative politeness

room. Negative politeness also involves more frequent use of other MITIGATING DEVICES, expressions that 'soften the blow', like *please, possibly, might, I'm sorry but . . .* etc.

In the next exercise we explore how Brown and Levinson's framework can be used to analyse directives.

Mitigating devices

✐ **EXERCISE**

8.5 You want to ask someone to lend you a stapler:

(a) Could you hint at this without saying anything? How?

(b) If you decide to say something, could you drop a hint rather than going 'on record' as asking the person for the stapler? Provide a utterance that could do this.

(c) If you do go on record as asking for the stapler, you are potentially threatening the other person's negative face by imposing on them and making it much harder for them to refuse. (You also risk losing your positive face if the hearer does not help you out.) You could go on record with a 'bald' request: Lend me your stapler. The imperative form leaves no room for doubt that this is a directive. Or, you could go on record but use a FACE-SAVING ACT, by phrasing your request in such a way that on the surface the other person is not directly ordered to perform the act. Here are two examples: Gotta stapler you can lend me? and Could you lend me your stapler? Which one uses a positive politeness strategy and which one uses a negative politeness strategy?

Face-saving act

(a) You could stack up the sheets of paper ready for the stapler and then start fumbling around in your drawer. In other words, you wait for the other person to offer. Perhaps you have had a similar experience in a restaurant where a friend has done a great deal of fumbling with their wallet or purse until you say Let me get this. (b) An off-record hint, the verbal equivalent of fumbling around in your drawer, would be something like I can't find my stapler or Where's my stapler gone? (c) In Brown and Levinson's analysis, Gotta stapler you can lend me? orients to positive politeness with its informality of pronunciation and phrasing, while Could you lend me your stapler? orients to negative politeness. The framework we have been using is summarized in Figure 1 on the following page.

Comment

■ Leech analysed politeness by the use of maxims. The **tact maxim: minimize cost to other; maximize benefit to other** helps distinguish requests from offers and influences the way we structure directives. The **approbation maxim:**

SUMMARY

minimize dispraise of other; maximize praise of other influences the way we structure representatives.

- Leech observed that the higher the cost for the hearer in a directive, or the greater the potential for dispraising the hearer in a representative, the more likely it is for the speaker to be indirect. However, the social distance between the speaker and hearer can also influence the degree of directness used.

- Brown and Levinson analyse politeness as showing awareness of the need to preserve **face** (public self-image).

- **Positive politeness** orients to preserving a person's self-image as an accepted, valued and liked member of a social group. **Negative politeness** orients to a person's self-image as an free individual who should not be imposed upon.

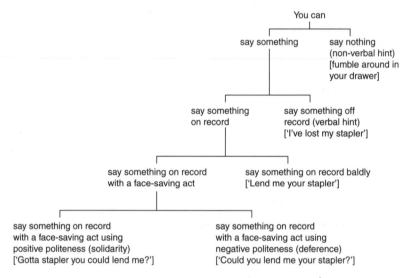

Figure 1   How to get someone to lend you a stapler (following Brown and Levinson, 1987)

FURTHER EXERCISES

8.6   Although Leech considered the tact maxim the most important influence on the way directives and commissives are phrased, and the approbation maxim the most crucial one for representatives, he has proposed several other politeness maxims. In this exercise we will look at two of them. In each section, follow the analysis directions. Then, looking overall at that section, see if you can formulate a maxim which might account for your choices.

Section A   In 1–3 there are three possible responses that Jane could make to Steve. Rank them in order of politeness, starting with the least polite.

1	Steve:	This is a great restaurant isn't it?
(a)	Jane:	Not really. I hate spicy food.
(b)	Jane:	It's pretty good value, but the food could have been less spicy.
(c)	Jane:	I'll say!

2	Steve:	I thought that movie was boring.
(a)	Jane:	So did I.
(b)	Jane:	That's rubbish! I loved it.
(c)	Jane:	Parts of it were a bit slow.

3	Steve:	Clinton's a fool.
(a)	Jane:	Well, he has done some foolish things.
(b)	Jane:	He is not!
(c)	Jane:	I'm sorry, I have to disagree with you.

Section B Decide which of the two utterances in each pair is more polite. Some examples also contain the previous speaker's utterance in square brackets which prompted the one you are analysing.

1(a) [Mike: Their singing was wonderful!]
     Annie: Yes, it was, wasn't it.
1(b) [Mike: Your singing was wonderful!]
     Annie: Yes, it was, wasn't it.

2(a) [Mike: I'm really grateful.]
     Annie: Don't mention it.
2(b) [Mike: I'm really grateful.]
     Annie: And so you should be. I helped a lot.

3(a) I brought this little gift for you.
3(b) I brought this large gift for you.

4(a) Would you like this sink cleaned up?
4(b) Would like me to clean up this sink?

8.7 Add to **Figure 1** to show the different ways you could get someone to stop blocking the television screen.

8.8 The following utterances could all be interpreted as directives. Does one member of each pair seem less polite than the other? What influenced your decision?

1(a) You must cut my lawn.
1(b) You should cut my lawn.
2(a) You will help me unload the car.
2(b) You might help me unload the car.

SUPPLE-
MENTARY
EXERCISES ✎

8.9   Below are three extracts from a course guide that I give my students. Pick out the different types of directives that I use and propose reasons for the choices I have made.

1   Failure to comply with these requirements is regarded by the Programme as a very serious offence and equivalent to cheating on an examination. Because of the serious consequences of plagiarism, make sure you have a copy of 'Guidelines for Students', read the section 'Conventions for Referencing' on p. 23, and if you still have any doubts, you must ask your tutor's advice *before* submitting your work.

2   If at any time you get into medical or personal difficulties which are likely to seriously affect your studies, please contact me, your personal tutor or the Programme Convenor as soon as possible so that we can explain your options and help you to find the best way forward.

3   The Reading List is by no means exhaustive and you are strongly encouraged to acquaint yourself with the child language books library. You will need to do a considerable amount of independent reading and study in order to complete your assignments successfully. Remember: Lectures and handouts are only guides to the reading not substitutes for it.

8.10   Five-year-old Sophie is having lunch at her friend Charlotte's house. Charlotte is three years old. Maureen is Charlotte's mother. Analyse the appropriateness of Sophie's directives using both Leech's politeness maxim approach and Brown and Levinson's positive and negative politeness framework. Does Sophie show evidence of using different types of directives appropriately? What about Charlotte's ability to comprehend different types of directives? What differences do you observe between Sophie's and Charlotte's attention to politeness? What might account for these differences?

Sophie: er can't undo this.
Charlotte: ask my Mum.
Sophie: em Maureen can you undo this please?

Sophie: oh I love Um Bongo (a soft drink). My mum never buys it.
Charlotte: A drop? A tiny bit? (offers some to Sophie)
Sophie: I haven't got a straw today.
Charlotte: Have one a ours.
Sophie: Ask your mum if we can have a straw.
Charlotte: Mummy. Mummy.
Sophie: Not while she's on the phone.
Charlotte: (shouting) Mummy. Mummy.
Sophie: It's to go (in a quiet voice) 'Mummy'.

Charlotte: (still shouting) Mum, I listening you.
Maureen.: Will you stop shouting at me!
Charlotte: (shouting) Mum, we wanna straw.
Maureen: OK. There's no need to shout.

Sophie: Don't like my pickle (eating a cheese and pickle sandwich).
Charlotte: Maureen.
Sophie: Don't tell her.
Charlotte: I am.
Sophie: Don't.
Charlotte: Mummy.
Maureen: What?
Charlotte: em Sophie doesn't like her pickle.
Maureen: That's all right.
Sophie: I like the cheese.

Sophie: Can I have some? (there's only one sheet of white drawing paper left)
Charlotte: OK I'll draw on something else.

💬 **DISCUSSION QUESTIONS**

8.11 Experiment with different intonation patterns on some of the direct directives in this unit. Can changes in tone of voice or word emphasis alter the level of politeness? You can also try this with the various responses in **Exercise 8.3** (representatives).

8.12 It has been suggested that, in our culture at least, negative politeness has the greatest influence on how we phrase directives while positive politeness has the greatest influence on how we phrase our representatives. Do you agree?

8.13 Observational studies of parents' conversations with their children have shown that there is a relatively high proportion of directive and instructive talk from the adults, either by blunt commands: *be careful, don't do that*, or by TALKING OVER. That is, talking about people in their presence and referring to them as *we* or *she/he*. The father's conversation with his daughter at the beginning of **Unit 1** is an illustration of this. Analyse the directive use in the following extracts. In what ways are they similar? What reasons can you propose for the similarity?

Talking over

1   C = Child, T.; M = Mother. C wants to turn on the lawn sprinklers. A researcher is present. (Adapted from Ervin-Tripp, 1979.)

C: Mommy.
M: T. has a little problem with patience. We're working on patience. What is patience, T.?
C: Nothing.

M: Come on.
C: I want to turn them on now.
M: What is patience? Can you remember?

2 A home help, her elderly client, R, and D, R's relative, are all in R's living room. The home help and D are discussing cakes which have been left for R. (Adapted from Atkinson and Coupland, 1988.)

D: They're in there and I'm hoping. They're in the fridge you see. I'm hoping she will go in there and take them and eat them.
Home help: That's right yeah don't waste . . .

FURTHER READING

In our discussion of Brown and Levinson's theories, we have concentrated on how the speaker orients to the hearer's face wants in directives. However, these authors discuss how the **speaker's** face wants can also influence the form of an utterance and how positive and negative politeness can be used to analyse other kinds of speech acts. In addition, their book has some fascinating data from other languages and cultures. See:

Brown and Levinson, 1987 (fairly challenging).

For an accessible discussion of Brown and Levinson's theories, see:

Yule, 1996, Chapter 7.

Leech proposes an interesting analysis of why the use of negative structures can give rise to different perceptions of politeness. Compare Will you sit down? and Won't you sit down? but Can you be quiet? with Can't you be quiet? See:

Leech, 1983, Chapters 5 and 6.

For introductions to children's acquisition of pragmatic skills and references to current work in this area, see:

Foster, 1990, Chapters 4.4 and 5.6
Gleason, 1997, Chapter 6.

MAKING SENSE

9

We look in more detail at the effects of context and at the role played by world knowledge in making sense of what we hear and read.

EXERCISE

9.1   I asked my students to read this passage:

> The procedure is quite simple. First you arrange things into different groups. Of course one pile may be sufficient depending on how much there is to do. If you have to go somewhere else due to lack of facilities that is the next step, otherwise you are pretty well set. It is important not to overdo things. That is, it is better to do too few things at once than too many. In the short run this may not seem too important but complications can easily arise. A mistake can be expensive as well. At first the whole procedure will seem complicated. Soon, however, it will just become another facet of life. It is difficult to foresee any end to the necessity for this task, in the immediate future, but then one can never tell. After the procedure is completed, one arranges the materials into different groups again. Then they can be put into their appropriate places. Eventually, they will be used once more and the whole cycle will have to be repeated. However that is a part of life.
>
> (Greene, 1986, p. 31)

Now, cover that passage and try to write down as much of it as you can remember.

Comment

This passage was used in a series of experiments by the psychologist J.D. Bransford to study the effects of context on our ability to make sense of what we hear and read. If you are like most people, I imagine you found it quite difficult to understand this passage and consequently it was quite difficult for you to remember what you had read. The problem is that the words are very general. What *things* have to be arranged? What do *facilities, procedure*, and *the appropriate places* refer to? Now read the passage again with some additional information: the title is 'Washing Clothes'. What we now find is that knowing what this text 'is about' allows us to use our knowledge about the world to infer what these words are referring to, and consequently to make sense of the text.

Of course, this text, which was especially written for experimental purposes, is quite artificial in that people do not usually talk or write quite so vaguely for so long. But look at this brief passage from a 'real' book:

> Any attempt consciously to bring about this enlargement is doomed to failure, and will successfully bring about those conditions of tension which it is essential to avoid. There are three regions or areas of expansion. Of these only one can be seen or felt.

> (Turner, 1977)

Out of context it is extremely difficult to make sense of this passage. (It comes from a book on voice production for actors, and more specifically, a section on avoiding a 'throaty tone'.)

In addition to helping us decide what general terms like *facilities* and *places* are referring to, the context of the discourse and our knowledge of the world help us to resolve ambiguity. Much of the language that we hear is technically ambiguous. We are usually unaware of this because, as we will see in the next exercise, the context and our expectations lead us so strongly to a particular interpretation.

EXERCISE ✎

9.2   Here are some newspaper headlines that have made it into collections of journalistic bloopers. For each of these, write down two possible interpretations. Decide what has caused the ambiguity. Then think about why one interpretation seemed more natural than the other.

(a)   Retired priest may marry Bruce Springsteen
(b)   Defendant's speech ends in long sentence
(c)   You can combat that feeling of helplessness with illegal drugs
(d)   Prison warden says inmates may have 3 guns
(e)   Rhode Island secretary excites furniture experts
(f)   Crowds rushing to see Pope trample 6 to death

Just like the hapless journalists, you might have found that you had
to work quite hard to find a second meaning for some of these headlines. Your knowledge about the world made one of the meanings
so obvious that you were temporarily 'blinded' to any other possible
interpretation.

(a) This could mean (1) A retired priest may perform Bruce
Springsteen's marriage ceremony, or (2) A retired priest
may become the spouse of Bruce Springsteen. This is a case
of LEXICAL AMBIGUITY because it arises from multiple
meanings of a particular word, the verb *to marry*. You probably found that your knowledge about Bruce Springsteen,
the role of priests in our society, and a perhaps unwarranted
assumption that the priest was a man made (1) the more
likely interpretation.

Lexical ambiguity

(b) This could mean (1) The defendant's speech results in a
long prison term, or (2) The defendant's speech finishes
with a long grammatical construction. This is another case
of lexical ambiguity. The verb *to end* has two slightly
different meanings, as does the noun *sentence*. Nevertheless, the word *defendant* sets up a courtroom context,
which makes interpretion (1) much more likely.

(c) This could mean (1) With illegal drugs, you can combat that
feeling of helplessness, or (2) That feeling of helplessness
with illegal drugs can be combated. Our knowledge of
society's views on illegal drugs leads us to expect that a
newspaper would probably have intended meaning (2).
This time the ambiguity has resulted not from a word with
more than one possible meaning, but from two alternative
interpretations of the grammatical structure. Did you
notice that the ambiguity can be remedied by using the
same words but producing two different sentence structures
which make the intended meaning unambiguous? This is
called SYNTACTIC AMBIGUITY. Sometimes we find cases
where there is both lexical and syntactic ambiguity as in the
famous *Guardian* headline in 1982: British left waffles on
Falklands.

Syntactic ambiguity

(d) This arises from the lexical ambiguity of *may*. As we saw
in **Further Exercise 8.8**, modal verbs can have two types
of meanings: EPISTEMIC which refers to how certain the
speaker is about the truth of the proposition, and DEONTIC
which refers to issues of permission or obligation. Our
knowledge of how prisons operate makes the deontic
interpretation much less likely.

Epistemic
Deontic

(e) This could mean (1) Rhode Island clerical worker excites
furniture experts, or (2) Rhode Island writing desk excites
furniture experts. This is another case of lexical ambiguity

but you may have found it a bit puzzling if your mental dictionary does not include 'writing desk' as one of the possible meanings of *secretary*. Did you notice how we interpret *excites* somewhat differently if we think that *secretary* refers to a woman rather than a man?

Ellipsis

(f)   This is another case of syntactic ambiguity. It could mean (1) Six are trampled to death by crowds rushing to see the Pope, or (2) The crowds are rushing to see the Pope trample six to death. Incidentally, did you notice how obvious it seemed that *six* referred to six **people**? ELLIPSIS, omitting words or even larger chunks of sentences, as in: (Do you want a cup of) Coffee? or I'll help. (clean up the kitchen), is so prevalent in discourse that we are usually not aware of how much information we are filling in from the context.

In the units on implicature, we were working mostly with pairs of utterances, from two different speakers. However, we also draw implicatures from a series of utterances from the same speaker (or writer). Since we assume that the speaker is adhering to the maxim of relevance, we assume that there is a connection between the utterances.

EXERCISE ✎

9.3   In each case, what implicatures do you have to draw for the utterances to be relevant to one another?

(a)   Wet feet? Look out for colds. Gargle with Listerine quick.

(b)   Is your teen just barely hanging on? Big Sky Montana is a great place for changes.

(c)   Tired of ordinary sport-utilities? Try the Subaru Forester.

(d)   Now there's a refrigerator that fits precisely into your renovation plans. Introducing the Monogram.

(e)   Introducing Microsun. A technological breakthrough.

(f)   Birds have sanctuaries. People have Hampton Inns.

Comment

Not surprisingly, the implicatures all allow the advertisers to make claims about their products without explicitly asserting them:

(a)   'Gargling with Listerine will prevent colds.' (In addition to implying 'Wet feet cause colds'.)

(b)   'Big Sky Montana (a psychiatric treatment centre) will change a situation where your teen is just barely hanging on.'

(c) 'The Subaru Forester is not an ordinary sports-utility vehicle.'

(d) 'The Monogram is a refrigerator that fits precisely into your renovation plans.'

(e) 'Microsun is a technological breakthrough.'

(f) 'Hampton Inns are sanctuaries.'

As you can see, implicatures can result from the relation between a series of phrases as well as a series of full sentences. (e) uses a format very typical in advertising where two noun phrases are linked by an implied *is/are*. Sometimes the link between two phrases requires even more elaborate inferencing, as in a rather unfortunate sign on the London Underground: **Terrorism. Substantial Rewards.**

Advertisements often have pictures in conjunction with the text. These pictures help to create a context which guides the interpretation. An advertisement for a dishwasher shows a woman floating in a swimming pool. The text reads **By removing crusty baked-on foods, our new Power Scour dishwasher virtually eliminates soaking. At least for dishes.**

✎ **EXERCISE**

9.4 Fill in the blank: There was an American president named James Polk, pronounced *poke* with a silent *l*. Similarly, *folk* is pronounced *foke* with a silent *l*, just as the white of an egg is pronounced ——.

Comment

Did you fall into the trap? Most people do. The expectations set up by the context (verbal context in this case) lead most people to forget that the yolk is the yellow part of an egg, not the white. Psychologists refer to this as the 'atmosphere effect'.

✎ **EXERCISE**

9.5 Would you consider signing this petition?

We ask that the government take measures to ensure the strict control or total elimination of dihydrogen monoxide. This chemical

- Is a major component of acid rain
- Can cause excessive sweating and vomiting
- Can cause death if accidentally inhaled
- Can cause severe burns in its gaseous state
- Contributes to soil erosion
- Decreases the effectiveness of automobile brakes
- Is found in patients with terminal cancer

Comment

This is a very striking example of the 'atmosphere effect'. The petition was part of a science project by an American high school student. He was investigating how scientific language can influence people's thinking. There actually is a chemical called dihydrogen monoxide. It does have all the alarming properties described in the petition. *Dihydrogen monoxide* is the scientific term for *water*. Look back at the petition. Do all those properties seem quite so alarming now?

EXERCISE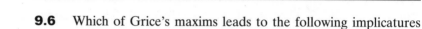

9.6   Which of Grice's maxims leads to the following implicatures in brackets?

  (a) What an elephant Jane is! ('Jane is clumsy')
  (b) Steve's a pig. ('Steve is greedy')

Comment

Assuming *Jane* in (a) and *Steve* in (b) are humans, these statements flout the maxim of quality. They are manifestly untrue. In order for us to assume that the speakers are still adhering to the co-operative

Metaphors

principle, we have to interpret these statements as METAPHORS. That is, figures of speech which imply a comparison between two concepts: 'Jane is like an elephant'; 'Steve is like a pig'. In (a) the further inference is 'Jane is like an elephant because she is clumsy'. In (b) 'Steve

Similes

is like a pig because he is greedy'. Technically, SIMILES are different from metaphors in that they make the comparison explicit, as in Jane is **like** an elephant, or Steve is **as** greedy **as** a pig. However, the underlying principle is the same, qualities are transferred from one concept to another. Or, to put it another way, one concept is being understood in terms of another related but different concept.

EXERCISE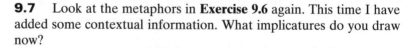

9.7   Look at the metaphors in **Exercise 9.6** again. This time I have added some contextual information. What implicatures do you draw now?

  (a) She's still mad at me. What an elephant Jane is!
  (b) Look at this room. Steve's a pig.

Comment

This time we infer in (a) 'Jane has a long memory', and in (b) 'Steve is messy'. In analysing metaphor, some authors emphasize the role played by the meaning overlap between the two concepts being compared. However, an ingenious study described in McCabe (1998) shows how, for a metaphor to work, the context in which the comparison is made can be much more important than any inherent similarities between the two concepts. American college students were given random pairs of nouns like *ache* and *autograph* and were asked to imagine a context where one could serve as a metaphor for the other. Here is one of the stories:

> My hometown doctor, Doc Wilson, was an old-fashioned country doctor. He knew all his patients, carefully and individually. Each **ache** was as uniquely identified with a patient as was his or her **autograph**. Doc Wilson knew you inside out.

SUMMARY

- The context of the discourse and our knowledge of the world help us to resolve potential ambiguity and vagueness in utterances, and to fill in missing information.
- In order to make sense of a series of utterances, we have to draw implicatures about the way the utterances are relevant to each other. Again, we are helped to draw these implicatures by world knowledge and the discourse context.
- The language itself can help set up a context which constrains our thinking, as we saw in the dihydrogen monoxide example. This is sometimes called 'atmosphere effect'.
- Context can play a powerful role in the interpretation of metaphors and similes.

🖉 **SUPPLE-MENTARY EXERCISES**

9.8   What has gone wrong in these headlines?

(a) Warranty aids home owners with defects
(b) Never withhold herpes infection from loved one
(c) Mondale's offensive looks hard to beat
(d) 5½ foot boa caught in toilet. Woman relieved
(e) Belfast man charged for Harrod's bomb
(f) Westinghouse gives robot rights to firm

9.9   Still on the subject of robots, what went wrong with this job advertisement for the University of Portsmouth? Research Assistant. Intelligent walking/climbing robot.

9.10   Play the metaphor game with your friends. Write a series of nouns, like *ache, autograph, fire hydrant, rubber band*, etc. on cards, and put them into a bag. Draw out two cards and create a story which uses one of the nouns as a metaphor for the other.

9.11   What implicature would you draw from an advertisement showing the Tower of London at night with the Beefeater Guard saying: We don't use guard dogs. They won't go inside. Manipulate the context so that an entirely different implicature would be drawn.

9.12   In psychology experiments about memory for texts, subjects often mistakenly think they heard Three turtles rested on a floating log and a fish swam beneath them when they had actually heard Three turtles rested on a floating log and a fish swam beneath it. Why?

9.13   In other psychology experiments, the sentences *The beer was warm* and *The chandeliers were shining brightly* took longer to read in their (b) context below than in their (a) context. Why do you think this might be the case?

  (a) We got some beer out of the car. The beer was warm.
  (b) We checked the picnic supplies. The beer was warm.

  (a) I walked into the garden. The chandeliers were shining brightly.
  (b) I walked into the sea. The chandeliers were shining brightly.

9.14   In **Supplementary Exercise 3.10**, you were asked to write advertisements that slipped in a series of claims via presupposition. Return to that set of claims and write advertisements for the same products, this time using implicature to slip in the claim. Use **Exercise 9.3** for ideas.

9.15   Ask people to read the following: I bought some imported Colombian coffee yesterday, but when I opened the package, there was a strange white powder inside. Then cover the sentence. Five minutes later ask them to write down the sentence they had read. Did they remember the sentence exactly or did they produce a paraphrase instead? Note down anything they omitted from the original sentence. Did the omissions contain information that could be inferred from the paraphrase? Note down anything they added in the remembered version. Did the additions contain information that could have been inferred from the original sentence?

9.16 It is sometimes said that language works by combining sounds into words, words into sentences and sentences into discourse. This implies that discourse is the 'product' of the previous steps. Think of all the ways that the context and purpose of the discourse affect how the language sounds, what the words mean, and how the sentences are structured.

DISCUSSION QUESTION

For more about the floating turtles and the warm beer, and how psychologists study the ways that we process discourse, see:

FURTHER READING

Garnham, 1985, Chapter 7.

In several of the units we mentioned how the use of gesture, body language and tone of voice can have significant effects on how we interpret utterances. If you would like to find out more about these aspects of communication, see:

Ellis and Beattie, 1986, especially Chapters 1–9.

For more about metaphor in relation to analysing written texts, see:

Thornborrow and Wareing, 1998, Chapter 4.

For more about metaphor as a way of making sense of the world, see:

Lakoff and Johnson, 1980.

10

EXPLORING PRAGMATICS: PROJECTS

PROJECT 1
Presupposition and implicature in advertising

There is currently a debate about whether advertising claims for cosmetics and vitamins should be treated as rigorously as claims for medicines. Make a collection of advertisements for each of these three types of products. Compare them on the degree to which they use presupposition, implicature and direct assertion to make claims about the benefits or effectiveness of the product. For example, look for differences in the frequency of implicatures that arise from the use of a series of phrases, rather than full sentences, as in Beta carotene. Nature's safest source of Vitamin A.

Advertisements tend to use the imperative form quite frequently. Sometimes this is to persuade us to: Buy X, or Visit our showroom, or Reserve a seat now. But the imperative also has another use in advertising. It carries the presupposition 'You will . . .' as in Find comfort and relief with X, or Look years younger instantly with Y. Look for differences in the frequency of imperative forms that trigger this type of presupposition.

You could expand this study or make a separate study of how modal verbs like *can*, *might*, *could*, and *may* are used to weaken claims for products. Again do you notice different frequencies of use for different types of products?

PROJECT 2
The directives adults use with children

Make a study of the types of directives that adults address to young children. If you can persuade a family with young children to let you tape record a family meal, you will get quite a lot of data. (In **Unit 8**, the extracts from Charlotte and Sophie's lunch were only a fraction of the entire transcript.) If this is not feasible, you can still gather quite a lot of data with a notepad and pen. Bus stops, supermarkets, toy stores and fast-food restaurants are all good places to hear parents talking to their children. You can look for the relative proportion of direct directives to indirect directives addressed to the child. Does this vary with the age of the child? Do mothers and fathers use different kinds of directives? Are there differences between the kinds of directives addressed to boys and those addressed to girls? If you can get data from two children interacting with an adult who is the parent of only one of them, you can look for differences between the directives parents use with their own children and those they use with other children.

Make a study of children's perceptions of what it is to talk politely. One way to do this is with two glove puppets. You can have both puppets ask for the same thing but using directives that differ in politeness. An example would be Puppet 1: Gimme some candy. Puppet 2: May I have some candy? Ask the child which puppet is being more polite. You should try to include directed acts that vary in their cost to the hearer, for example Clean the floor vs. Pass the sugar, as well as those which vary in their degree of directness. This study would be especially interesting if you compare two or more children of different ages, a 3-year-old and a 7-year-old for example.

    You could also extend the study by including representatives with varying degrees of politeness. How stupid you are! vs. How clever you are! vs. How clever I am! etc. If you fancy yourself as playwright, construct little dramas for the puppets which involve adherence to or violation of the agreement maxim.

**PROJECT 3
Children's
perceptions of
polite ways of
talking**

The basis of much humour is the violation of our expectations about how people should behave. Using Leech's politeness maxims, make a detailed analysis of Basil Fawlty's verbal rudeness as well as his exaggerated but often doomed attempts to flatter his guests. Three scripts from the series appear in Cleese and Booth (1977).

**PROJECT 4
Basil Fawlty
and politeness
maxims**

Once when I was visiting the USA, I walked into a shop that sells jeans and casual clothes. The young sales assistant was a model of positive politeness: Hi! How are you today? Fine, thanks, I answered. With strangers we normally expect the exchange to end there, but she then added That's great! That's real great! I later learned that the assistants working for this chain of shops are trained to greet customers like this not only to foster a friendly image of the store but also to deter shoplifters. Apparently, if you know you have been noticed, you are less likely to shoplift. On the other hand, have you ever been in a store where the shop assistants are models of negative politeness, even asking permission to make an offer as in May I help you, madam? Spend a day in stores with a notepad and pencil. Make an analysis of the politeness strategy that different stores use.

**PROJECT 5
Positive and
negative
politeness in
stores**

PROJECT 6
The use of
presupposition
in political
debates and
interviews

Neil Kinnock to John Major: Doesn't the prime minister recall saying in Zimbabwe last year that tax reductions in the March budget would be fool's gold?

Dennis Skinner to Margaret Thatcher: Does the prime minister regret using a three line whip as a guillotine on the Single European Act?

(Quoted in Simpson, 1993)

Do you notice how the presuppositions triggered by Doesn't the prime minister recall ... and Does the prime minister regret ... 'position' the hearer to admit to the presupposed act whether they answer the question 'yes' or 'no'. Another tactic that is sometimes used in interviews is to ask questions of the type How outraged are you by the government's decision? which presupposes that the interviewee is outraged. It takes a lot of work to deny every presupposition in a question, and consequently many of them go unchallenged. This can make presupposition a powerful tool in political debates and interviews.

Make video recordings of political debates and interviews. How prevalent is this tactic? Can you tell what the interviewers' points of view are by the presuppositions they use? You could extend your analysis of pragmatics, politics and point of view by looking at the types of verbs used to refer to speech acts. The honourable member has stated/admitted/confessed that ...

PROJECT 7
Analysing
written
directives

In **Supplementary Exercise 8.9** you analysed the directives I used in my course guides. You can broaden your investigation by collecting a series of course guides and other instructions to students, including notices on bulletin boards and office doors. What factors can you identify that cause variations in the style of directives used? Other sources of written directives are information on passports and licences (my US passport is a symphony of modal verbs), membership rules and information distributed by clubs, especially health clubs.

ETHICAL
GUIDELINES
FOR PROJECT
WORK

- Although it is all right to use a pen and notepad to record speech that you hear in a public place, you should never tape record people without their knowledge, even in public places.
- When writing up your project, never identify your informants by their real names. You can refer to them either by initials or by a pseudonym.
- Whenever you are working with children, make sure that you obtain permission from either their parents or their teachers (if you are collecting data in a school).
- When working with children you should explain the nature of your study to their parent or teacher and emphasize

that your goal is not to evaluate individual children in any way, but to learn about children's pragmatic development in general.

- Remember that children are people! If they become tired or want to discontinue the activity despite your gentle encouragement, you must respect their wishes. You may have to take a break or return at another time to finish collecting your data.

ANSWERS TO FURTHER EXERCISES

UNIT 1

1.7 (a) Pragmatics. It concerns **speaker** meaning.

(b) Sentence semantics. Jane is giving a semantic paraphrase of a sentence in Steve's lease.

(c) Pragmatics. The parent is commenting not on the literal meaning of **Where are your shoes, young man?** but on what **she** meant by using that utterance. The child has misinterpreted her request for action as a request for information.

(d) Lexical semantics. Faye is clarifying what a word means by providing a SYNONYM (a word with a similar meaning), *mournful*, and an ANTONYM (a word with the opposite meaning), *cheerful*.

Synonym
Antonym

(e) Pragmatics. The sentence *Life is a tale told by an idiot* has the semantic paraphrase *Life is a story told by someone with diminished mental capacity*. But Sarah is giving a pragmatic paraphrase. That is, what the **speaker** meant by uttering those words, not what the words literally mean. This kind of figurative language is called a METAPHOR. Here, *life* is being implicitly compared to something else, *a tale told by an idiot*.

Metaphor

1.8 Here are some sample paraphrases:

(a) *Her mother is unhappy.*
SP: *Her mother is sad.* (word substitution *unhappy* replaced by a synonym *sad*)

(b) *My friend loathes string beans.*
SP1: *My pal hates string beans.* (word substitution, *friend* replaced by *pal*, and *loathe* replaced by *hate*)
SP2: *String beans are loathed by my friend.* (change of sentence structure from ACTIVE to PASSIVE)

Active
Passive

84

> SP3: *String beans are hated by my friend.* (word substitution, *loathe* replaced by *hate*, and change of sentence structure from active to passive)

(c) *I'll look for that book right now.*
> SP: *I'll search for that book immediately.* (word substitution, *look* replaced by *search* and *right now* replaced by *immediately*)

(d) *Steve hugged Jane.*
> SP1: *Jane was hugged by Steve.* (change of sentence structure from active to passive)
> SP2: *Steve gave Jane a hug.* (change in sentence structure)

2.7 (a) Analytically 'true' because of the meaning relationship between *hamster* and *mammal*. A hamster is a kind of mammal.

(b) This cannot be designated as 'true' or 'false' unless you know whether my cousin is male or female, and how old she/he is (extra-linguistic information).

(c) Unless you happen to refer to all female humans as *girls* regardless of their age, technically this cannot be designated as 'true' or 'false' unless you know how old my sister is (extra-linguistic information).

(d) Analytically 'true' because of the meaning relationship between *sister* and *female*. All sisters are female (unlike all cousins).

(e) Analytically 'false' because saying that a rock is female entails that it is a creature. But remember, this is 'false' only from a strictly semantic point of view. From a pragmatic point of view, anything is possible. Uttered in the context of watching a cartoon about the adventures of Papa and Mama Rock and all their baby rocks, this could be either 'true' or 'false' depending on the rock in question.

(f) This cannot be designated as 'true' or 'false' unless you know something about the particular tortoise that I saw (extra-linguistic information).

(g) This cannot be designated as 'true' or 'false' unless you know the eating habits of my particular cat (extra-linguistic information).

(h) Analytically 'true' because of the meaning relationship between *sick* and *well* (*sick* means *not well*).

UNIT 2

2.8 Here are some sample entailments.

(a) *My sister-in-law grows roses.* → *My sister-in-law grows flowers.*
My sister-in-law grows roses. ↔ *Roses are grown by my sister-in-law.*

    (b)   *Steve is furious.* → *Steve is not calm.*
           Steve is furious. ↔ *Steve is very angry.*

    (c)   *Tom sold a computer to Mark.* → *Tom sold something to Mark.*
           Tom sold a computer to Mark. ↔ *Mark bought a computer from Tom.*

    (d)   *My brother repaired my car.* → *My brother repaired a vehicle.*
           My brother repaired my car. ↔ *My brother fixed my car.*

UNIT 3

3.7 (a) 'The defendant had bought a knife.'
    (b) 'You have been selling cocaine.'
    (c) 'A bracelet was stolen' and 'The bracelet belonged to you'.
    (d) 'The woman was murdered' and 'She left the office'.
    (e) 'The driver ran the red light.'
    (f) 'You telephoned your lover.'
    (g) 'You have been an active gang member.'
    (h) 'You left the scene of the crime' and 'A crime had been committed.'

3.8 (a) 'Blasee is effective' and 'There is a secret to Blasee's effectiveness'.
    (b) 'The packs are distinctive' and 'Bippo is stocked locally' and 'There is a pack that's just right for you'.
    (c) 'All the puffiness and wrinkles will disappear'.
    (d) 'It is possible to protect against water spots' and 'The protection has been increased'.
    (e) 'Before you could not get a really crisp professional finish'.
    (f) 'It has been discovered how to perfect skin in three ways' and 'Each of these discoveries is potent' and 'The formula is gentle'.

UNIT 4

4.6 (a) 'I have a boyfriend' = presupposition. (This existential presupposition requires no previous utterance to arrive at the inference.)
    (b) 'You are laughing at me' = presupposition. (This is a conventional assumption in a Wh- question and requires no previous utterance to arrive at this kind of inference.)
    (c) 'She didn't have any supper' = implicature. (It requires shared knowledge between the speaker and the hearer as to whether anyone else could have given her supper.)
    (d) 'Mike is engaged' = implicature. (It needs non-linguistic knowledge about the custom of buying an engagement ring and also needs the context of a previous utterance. Look how the implicature would change if the previous utterance were **Is Mike giving his mother a present?**)

(e) There is some debate about this one, but usually the inference 'I tried to pass the exam' is analysed as a presupposition on the basis that it requires no previous utterance to draw it. It also holds up under negation. For most people's definition of *manage*, I didn't manage to pass the exam, likewise presupposes that 'I tried to pass the exam'. When a specific word (*manage* in this case) triggers a presupposition, it is sometimes called a LEXICAL PRESUPPOSITION.

Lexical presupposition

(f) Again, this is a bit tricky, but 'I didn't finish the report' is normally analysed as an implicature. I could continue the utterance by saying I started it and I finished it without sounding contradictory because the original utterance only **implied** that I hadn't finished it. (We will look at this 'test' for an implicature in more detail in the next unit.)

4.7 (a) Mike has not observed the **quality maxim** (be truthful). This is a **violation**, because, assuming that Annie does not know the answer already, it would not be obvious to her that Mike is telling a lie.

(b) Mike has not observed the **clarity maxim**. This is a **violation**, because Mike is not deliberately speaking unclearly.

(c) This is **flouting** of the **relevance maxim**. If meat had been the main course, Annie would probably draw the implicature 'Mike didn't like the dinner'.

(d) This is a **flouting** of the **quantity maxim**. The student is providing much more information than is normally required in this situation. If I were the teacher I might draw the implicature that 'The student was bored and "counting the minutes" until the end of the lecture'.

(e) Since this is obviously untrue, we have a **flouting** of the **quality maxim**. Student B can only be co-operative if we interpret this as a dramatic way of saying 'I'm very tired'. This type of figurative exaggeration is called HYPERBOLE.

Hyperbole

(f) This is a case of **flouting** the **clarity maxim**. (Compare this to (b) where Mike could not help being unclear.) Most people would draw the implicature 'I'm a bit dubious about drinking that cocktail'.

5.6 (a) 'Her central heating is broken' = presupposition. Note the contradiction that results from the cancellation: She discovered that her central heating was broken but it wasn't broken.

UNIT 5

(b) 'I don't like it hot' = a scalar implicature. It can be cancelled without sounding odd: I like it warm. No, actually, I like it hot.

(c) 'The necklace is not beautiful' = implicature. Here's an example of a cancellation: The bracelet is beautiful and in fact so is the necklace.

(d) 'No' = implicature. Here's an example of a cancellation: Tom's away, but Mark came over and painted it for me.

(e) 'It's not Steve's sweater' = implicature. Here's an example of a cancellation: There's a sweater on the sofa but it's mine.

(f) 'Mary hates the dentist' = implicature. Here's an example of a cancellation: We're going to the D-E-N-T-I-S-T and she's hoping he'll ask her out.

(g) 'Eric fixed it' = presupposition. Note the contradiction that results from the cancellation: When did Eric fix it even though he didn't fix it?

5.7 Examples (b), (c) and (e) are generalized implicatures. Examples (d) and (f) are particularlized implicatures. In (d) you would need particular knowledge about Tom and Gabriela. To what degree is Gabriela dependent on Tom to get the kitchen painted? In (f) the original implicature is more likely if Mary is a small child and is actually present in the room. If Mary is an adult and out of earshot, Annie could be humorously implying that Mary has a secret crush on the dentist.

UNIT 6

6.7 (a) No. The verb is performative but the subject is not in the first person. You hereby congratulate me sounds distinctly odd.

(b) No. The speaker cannot envy someone simply by speaking. So, *envy* is not a performative verb. Note the oddity of I hereby envy you.

(c) Yes. The verb is performative since it is possible to give an order by speaking. The subject is the speaker. The verb is in the simple present tense. I hereby command you to put out that cigarette sounds stilted but not odd.

(d) No. The verb is performative but it is in the past tense. Note the oddity of I hereby warned you not to go.

(e) No. The verb is not performative. You cannot put toys away by speaking. The 'hereby' test produces: Hereby put your toys away.

(f) No. The subject is in the first person and the verb is in the simple present tense. But, while convincing can be done by speaking, it is not under the control of the speaker and is therefore not a performative verb. Note the oddity of We hereby convince everyone with our arguments.

6.8 A likely possibility would be:

LOCUTION: Steve uttered the words, I was rude, which can be semantically paraphrased as: 'I was ill-mannered', with *I* referring to *Steve*.
ILLOCUTION: Steve performed the **act of apologizing** to Jane for having interrupted her.
PERLOCUTION: Jane accepted Steve's apology.

7.10 In **Exercise 7.2**:

(a) Coco's sick is a surface representative. But it could be taken as a 'hint' for Steve to take her to the vet, making it an indirect directive.
(b) What's the weather like in Dallas? seems to be a true rogative.
(c) The garage is a mess is a representative.

In **Exercise 7.3**:

(d) You've thrown away the paper is a representative, but in this context it seems to be functioning more specifically as an accusation. Dave seems to have drawn this inference since he then apologizes.
(e) A likely analysis here is that I got a new Nintendo game is a statement (a kind of representative), perhaps with an element of boasting.

These dialogues illustrate how speech acts often come in pairs: request/offer, question/answer, accusation/apology, statement/query. In (c) were you surprised by Faye's response? It seems as if Ed might have been following the same strategy as Jane in dialogue (a). Unfortunately, it resulted in a rather blunt directive from Faye rather than an offer to clean up the garage.

7.11 (a) Although this includes the polite addition of *please*, this is still a direct directive. It has an imperative structure and it fulfils the felicity conditions for a directive. The speaker has the right to make this request, and the child is capable of carrying it out. The requested action is not something that has already happened or would happen anyway. The action is desirable to the speaker.

(b) This is an indirect directive. It is a surface representative (declarative structure) but violates a key felicity condition for representatives: a representative should state information that is not already known to the hearer. Note that the statement about making the bed mentions an act that is desirable to the speaker and which has not happened yet, two key felicity conditions for a directive. Note also that the other conditions for a directive are also fulfilled.

(c) This is a pseudo-directive. Although it has an imperative form, the 'directed' act is potentially much more desirable for the hearer than the speaker. And besides, there is no use directing someone not to do an act which they have just done. In fact, we recognize this as a common alternative to You're welcome (an expressive).

UNIT 8

8.6 *Section A* Most people rank the utterances like this:

1(a) Jane: Not really. I hate spicy food.
 (b) Jane: It's pretty good value, but the food could have been less spicy.
 (c) Jane: I'll say!

2(b) That's rubbish! I loved it.
 (c) Parts of it were a bit slow.
 (a) So did I.

3(b) He is not!
 (c) I'm sorry, I have to disagree with you.
 (a) Well, he has done some foolish things.

Agreement maxim

What emerges here is Leech's AGREEMENT MAXIM: **minimize disagreement between self and other; maximize agreement between self and other.** Blunt rejection of another person's assertions as in 1(a), 2(b) and 3(b) is usually seen as impolite. Brown and Levinson would say that this threatens positive face as it implies that the speaker does not share or value the hearer's beliefs. So, we often try find at least a basis for partial agreement as in 1(b), 2(c) and 3(a). Have you noticed than when we must disagree with someone, we often mitigate this by apologizing for it as 3(c)?

Modesty maxim

Section B Most people rank the (a) utterances in each pair as more polite. What emerges here is Leech's MODESTY MAXIM: **minimize praise; maximize dispraise of self.** Compare How clumsy I am! with How talented I am! An explanation for the difference between 4(a) and 4(b) is that in 4(a) the speaker suppresses the role as a generous benefactor and therefore appears more modest.

8.7 Here are some possibilities:

Say nothing: but keep shifting around on the sofa or craning your neck.
Say something off record: This is a really exciting programme.
Say something on record baldly: Move out of the way.
Say something on record with a face-saving act using positive politeness: You make a better door than a window, or How about moving over just a teensy bit.
Say something on record with a face-saving act using negative politeness: Would you mind moving just a bit?

8.8 Most people perceive the (a) member of each pair to be less polite. The MODAL VERBS, *can, could, should, will, would, must, may, might* convey not only varying degrees of certainty about the truth of a statement (He must have failed his exam vs. He might have failed his exam), but also varying degrees of obligation on the subject of the sentence. These utterances are all indirect directives since they have a declarative rather than an imperative form, but the (a) utterances seem much less indirect than the (b) utterances. The use of high obligation modals like *will* and *must* in combination with the hearer as subject *(you)*, and the fact that the acts mentioned involve benefit for the speaker and cost for the hearer, make them nearly as blunt as imperatives.

BIBLIOGRAPHY

(References marked with * are particularly suitable for beginners)

Anobile, R. (1972) *Why a Duck*, London: Studio Vista.

Ash, R. (1985) *Howlers*, Horsham: Ravette.

Atkinson, K. and Coupland, N. (1988) 'Accommodation as ideology', *Language and Communication* 8: 321–7.

Austin, J.L. (1975) *How to Do Things with Words* (2nd edn), (J. Urmson and M. Sbisa eds) Oxford: Oxford University Press.

Bishop, D. (1997) *Uncommon Understanding*, Hove: Psychology Press.

Blakemore, D. (1992) *Understanding Utterances*, Oxford: Blackwell.

Brown, P. and Levinson, S. (1987) *Politeness: Some Universals in Language Usage*, Cambridge: Cambridge University Press.

Cleese, J. and Booth, C. (1977) *Fawlty Towers*, London: Contact Publications.

Cooper, G. (ed.) (1987) *Red Tape Holds up New Bridge*, New York: Perigee.

Coulthard, M. (1985) *An Introduction to Discourse Analysis* (2nd edn), London: Longman.

Crystal, D. (1987) *The Cambridge Encyclopedia of Language,* Cambridge: Cambridge University Press.*

Ellis, A. and Beattie, G. (1986) *The Psychology of Language and Communication*, Hove: Lawrence Erlbaum Associates.*

Ervin-Tripp, S. (1979) 'Children's verbal turntaking', in E. Ochs and B. Schieffelin (eds) *Developmental Pragmatics*, New York: Academic Press.

Foster, S. (1990) *The Communicative Competence of Young Children*, London: Longman.*

Garnham, A. (1985) *Psycholinguistics: Central Topics*, London: Routledge.

Gleason, J. (ed.) (1997) *The Development of Language* (4th edn), Boston: Allyn & Bacon.*

Greene, A. (1969) *Pullet Surprises*, Glenview: Scott, Foresman & Co.

Greene, J. (1986) *Language Understanding: A Cognitive Approach*, Buckingham: Open University Press.

Grice, P. (1989) *Studies in the Way of Words*, Cambridge, MA: Harvard University Press.

Hurford, J. and Heasley, B. (1988) *Semantics: A Coursebook*, Cambridge: Cambridge University Press.*

Labov, W. and Fanshel, D. (1977) *Therapeutic Discourse: Psychotherapy as Conversation*, New York: Academic Press.

Lakoff, G. and Johnson, M. (1980) *The Metaphors We Live By*, Chicago: University of Chicago Press.

Leech, G. (1981) *Semantics*, Harmondsworth: Penguin.

Leech, G. (1983) *Principles of Pragmatics*, London: Longman.

Levinson, S. (1983) *Pragmatics*, Cambridge: Cambridge University Press.

McCabe, A. (1998) 'Sentences combined: text and discourse', in J. Gleason (ed.) *Psycholinguistics* (2nd edn), Fort Worth: Harcourt Brace.

Obler, L. and Menn, L. (1982) *Exceptional Language and Linguistics*, New York: Academic Press.

Petras, R. and Petras, K. (1994) *The 776 Stupidest Things Ever Said*, London: Michael O'Mara Books.

Post, E. (1922) *Etiquette* (replica edition published in 1969), New York: Funk & Wagnalls.

Searle, J. (ed.) (1971) *The Philosophy of Language*, Oxford: Oxford University Press.

Searle, J. (1979) *Expression and Meaning*, Cambridge: Cambridge University Press.

Simpson, P. (1993) *Language, Ideology and Point of View*, London: Routledge.*

Sperber, D. and Wilson, D. (1986) *Relevance: Communication and Cognition*, Oxford: Blackwell.

Stubbs, M. (1983) *Discourse Analysis*, Oxford: Blackwell.

Thornborrow, J. and Wareing, S. (1998) *Patterns in Language*, London: Routledge.*

Turner, J. (1977) *Voice and Speech in the Theatre* (3rd edn), London: Pitman.

Yule, G. (1996) *Pragmatics*, Oxford: Oxford University Press.*

INDEX

The page numbers in **bold** indicate where a KEY WORD is defined and/or illustrated by examples. Authors' names which appear in this index are those specifically mentioned in the text or exercises for Units 1–10 (*see also* Bibliography).